▪ Fair Trial

Safeguards in European Law

Editor
Ian Mason
of Lincoln's Inn,
Barrister

𝔗𝔥𝔢 𝔥𝔬𝔫𝔬𝔲𝔯𝔞𝔟𝔩𝔢 𝔖𝔬𝔠𝔦𝔢𝔱𝔶 𝔬𝔣 𝔏𝔦𝔫𝔠𝔬𝔩𝔫'𝔰 𝔍𝔫𝔫

© The Honourable Society of Lincoln's Inn 1999

Published by
The Honourable Society of Lincoln's Inn
Lincoln's Inn
London WC2A 3TL

ISBN 1 902558 31 6

All rights reserved. No part of this publication may be reproduced, stored in a retrieval system, or transmitted, in any form or by any means, electronic, mechanical, photocopying, recording or otherwise, without the prior written permission of the publishers.

Produced for The Honourable Society of Lincoln's Inn by Palladian Law Publishing Ltd, Beach Road, Bembridge, Isle of Wight PO35 5NQ

Typeset by Heath Lodge Publishing Services
Printed in Great Britain by The Book Company Ltd

· Contents ·

Foreword by Ian Mason	v
Introduction by Paul Heim CMG	ix
The Right to a Fair Trial in European Law b*y Francis Jacobs QC*	1
Unpacking the Human Rights Act *by Lord Lester QC*	21
European Law and Criminal Proceedings *by George Carman QC*	34
European Law and Civil Proceedings *by Peter Duffy QC*	45
A Judicial Perspective of the Impact of European Law *by The Rt Hon Lord Justice Walker*	58
List of Cases Cited	72
Index	75

· Foreword ·

Ian Mason*

We live in an age when ancient institutions are under challenge on all sides and where in order to survive they have to demonstrate their continued relevance and usefulness. Lincoln's Inn, like all the remaining Inns of Court, is a medieval institution which has served the common law for over 600 years. During all that time it has been the professional home of lawyers and judges: a home not merely for residence and dining, but also for professional practice and development.

The Inns are essentially professional and teaching institutions. Their tradition is one of learning and teaching; of the most eminent in the profession meeting with students and practitioners to consider the common law and its development and to debate developing points and themes. In this way, over the centuries, the Inns became a professional university of the law and of advocacy.

The conference held at Lincoln's Inn in October 1998 was entirely in keeping with this tradition. Participants included a judge advocate of the European Court of Justice, a judge elect of the European Court of Human Rights, a Lord Justice of Appeal, judges of the High and circuit courts, academic lawyers, practitioners and students gathered to hear and discuss the law of England and of Europe as it is developing and is likely to develop in the world in which they live and practise.

The themes addressed are not unfamiliar to the Inns of Court. All the great themes of the common law have been debated here for centuries. Central to them are concepts of freedom and of justice, of the proper roles of state and individual, and of the role of the law in maintaining a proper balance of freedom and power in the life of a nation. Perhaps the single most dominant theme of all has been to ensure that the laws of the state are consistent with the ever-expanding freedom of a free and law abiding people.

---

* a barrister of Lincoln's Inn, practising at 2 King's Bench Walk Chambers.

There has never been a challenge to compare with the challenge of Europe. The growing power and influence of European law challenges every principle of the common law. A whole new system of law is developing out of the civil law tradition of continental Europe and the lessons learnt from the terrible events of the 20th century. But the new system must deal with the same problems as the old ones. It must find a balance between executive power and private freedom, between state and individual, which is in harmony with the understanding of the age and with the highest human aspirations for justice and freedom.

It should not be surprising to find the Inns of Court, and those trained in the common law, rising to this challenge and that was the aim of this conference. Centred on the theme of fair trial, the matrix in which the rights of state and individual are determined, the conference has inevitably focussed on human rights and the significance of the European Convention on Human Rights and the Human Rights Act. This was a conference of practical lawyers dealing with highly practical issues and trying to envisage the solutions to the ancient legal problems appropriate to the new legal world.

The new and developing law of Europe is as much part of the world of the Inns of Court as any developments in the law have ever been, and the fact that the Inn can attract the most distinguished British and European lawyers as participants is testimony to the continued relevance and importance of the Inns to the legal life of Britain and of Europe. So long as they continue to fulfill their role as institutions of learning, teaching and practice, the Inns will continue to thrive.

It is no small part of the tradition that this conference has been organised and staffed almost entirely by volunteer members of the Inn, from Bench, Bar and from the student body, all giving time, energy and expertise to make the event a great success. Unqualified thanks are due to all those who have participated, particularly our distinguished speakers, those who chaired the workshops (Sir Maurice Drake DFC, The Hon Mr Justice Charles, Roy Amlot QC, Anthony Grabiner QC and Cherie Booth QC) and that energetic body of new entrants to the profession who did so much of the work to prepare the workshops and assist in running the event. The work did not stop there and thanks are also due to those who assisted in preparing this volume for publication, especially The Hon Mrs Hilary Winstone who transcribed the recordings of the lectures here published, to David Scorey, who edited various of its parts of them, to Sue Phillips, untiring Deputy Under-Treasurer with special responsibility for education, not only for her total determination that it should be published, but also for carrying the whole event. Finally thanks are due to Paul Heim CMG for his vision and leadership throughout and to his steering committee, which included The Hon Mr Justice Lightman, the late Peter Duffy QC, Matthew Nicklin and Parosha Chandran.

Ian Mason

· Introduction ·

Paul Heim CMG*

Before introducing Advocate General Jacobs, let me thank the European Commission for its sterling support of the European law conference which this evening inaugurates.

The Commission's encouragement for the teaching of European law fits perfectly with the vocation of the Inns of Court, which for centuries have brought judges, barristers and students together, in a collegiate search for that knowledge whose aim is justice.

If British justice is admired abroad, it is much because of the evident confidence which reigns between Bench and Bar, fostered through these Inns of Court.

Lincoln's Inn is proud of its long association with that broad body of common and treaty law which we call European law. We are proud too of the contribution to that law of members of this Inn. When the United Kingdom joined the European Communities in 1973, the first judicial voice to bring together English and European law in Luxembourg was that of our Past-Treasurer, Sir Jean-Pierre Warner, then Advocate General. The Advocate General in Lux-embourg has a key role, pronouncing individually, independently and in open court, in each case.

In those early days at his right hand was none other than Francis Jacobs, now himself Advocate General.

The Inn is proud to have amongst its members so many others who have contributed to European law in its wider sense. Some are present here today, Sir John Freeland, past Judge in Strasbourg, and Nicolas Bratza, the present Judge. Lord Lester of Herne Hill will be speaking tomorrow.

The list is long. The Commission will know that what we now call fundamental rights have been defended by members of this Inn over the centuries. In fact, the first scheme for unifying Europe through justice

---

* Past Registrar of the European Court of Justice.

was worked out in these halls in the late 17th century, by the great libertarian, Penn. Peace, justice, meetings of the representatives of States, the peaceful settlement of disputes, majority voting, even a European civil service, all are foreseen by him. Official languages are established – French and Latin.

In his own trial, of course, Penn appealed to those rights as enshrined in common law, codified by Magna Carta and, as he said, confirmed by later statutes.

Were he speaking now, he would say that those rights had been reconfirmed in this century, by the European Convention on Human Rights, and by the general principles of law applied by the European Court in Luxembourg.

If European law innovates, it also confirms. Even the principle of proportionality, which we used to call an importation, was expressed in that great Charter:

> "No man will we amerce greatly for a small fault, but according to the nature of the fault."

It is gratifying that Sir Thomas More, whose name we have given to these lectures, has also lent his name to the new court building in Luxembourg. I must say that I never thought, when I arranged for that building to be constructed, that it would bear the name of our greatest, though not our only, European lawyer.

The success of this conference will be assured by the quality of the speakers, and of the attendance. The Commission will have noted that every level of national and European jurisdiction is represented. Much work has gone into presentation, and I must mention the names of Peter Duffy, without whom this event would not have taken place, Sue Phillips, whose contribution is always beyond praise and her team in the Treasury Office. A host of young students and barristers have helped, as did our man in Brussels who had the idea first.

The most important, Francis Jacobs, Barrister, Author, European civil servant, Referendaire, Professor, Silk, Advocate General, is no stranger to this Inn nor to any of you. He is warmly welcomed here, for what he is, what he has achieved and for what he is about to tell us.

Paul Heim CMG

The Right to a Fair Trial in European Law

Sir Thomas More Lecture

Francis G. Jacobs*

1. Introduction

As this is the inaugural Sir Thomas More lecture, it seems appropriate to start with a few words about Thomas More himself, a perennially fascinating man, who lived at the very transition from the medieval to the modern world; who bridged the worlds of religion and humanism, of private devotion and of public service. A man of principle in public life, who paid for his principles with his head. Described by his close friend, Erasmus, unforgettably, as a man for all seasons. Erasmus, himself perhaps the greatest scholar of his age, in an age which embraced the whole of Europe, which shared a common heritage and even a common language, also used less complimentary language to describe his friend. Erasmus seems to have been not entirely happy that More devoted his talents to the law. More was admitted as a student at Lincoln's Inn just over 500 years ago, and was kept by his father on "a very small allowance". Erasmus was obliged to recognise that More's mind was so extraordinarily sharp and subtle that he made the perfect advocate. He soon came to exercise judicial functions: as an under-sheriff, he acquired a reputation for quick and fair decisions; he was so efficient that, even before the Woolf reforms were dreamt of, it was said that no one promoted justice in London more effectively; and – another point of topical interest – he often remitted the fees which litigants were generally obliged to pay.

---

* Advocate General, Court of Justice of the European Communitites

He occupied several posts at Lincoln's Inn: as pensioner (*i.e.* financial administrator), as butler, as marshal, as autumn reader, and as Lent reader. As Lord Chancellor, he sometimes sat in the hall of Lincoln's Inn.

As those of you who have visited the European Court of Justice will know - and we are very pleased to welcome regular visits from Lincoln's Inn - Thomas More is remembered there too. The first extension of the Court's buildings was called after Erasmus; the second - following a survey of staff opinion - is called the Thomas More building. I hope it is not entirely inappropriate to use the names of those great Europeans from the past for these modern buildings. If you disregard the buildings - whatever their architectural merits or demerits - and look at the institution, there does emerge the beginnings of what I think can be called a developing European legal culture.

This culture is well illustrated by the programme for this conference - put together by Paul Heim, who has first-hand experience of both Strasbourg and Luxembourg and is now the embodiment of European law at Lincoln's Inn. The programme demonstrates vividly the impact of both streams of European law on English law - on the one hand, the European Convention on Human Rights and the Strasbourg case law; on the other hand, European Community law and the case law of the European Court of Justice.

My own contribution in this lecture will necessarily be a mere overview, an attempt to see some of the basic ideas and some connections, which will be explored more fully, and more professionally, in the sessions of the conference.

2. Access to justice under the European Convention on Human Rights

The right of access to a court is not as such guaranteed by the Convention. Article 6 provides by the first sentence of paragraph 1:

> "In the determination of his civil rights and obligations or of any criminal charge against him, everyone is entitled to a fair and public hearing within a reasonable time by an independent and impartial tribunal established by law."

In a landmark judgment in *Golder* v *United Kingdom*[1], decided in 1975, the European Court of Human Rights held that Article 6(1)

---

1 (1975) 1 EHRR 525.

guaranteed the right of access to a court. Moreover the right was to be available to a person serving a sentence of imprisonment in England – notwithstanding the fact that the nature of English civil proceedings made the exercise of that right difficult in practice. In that case a convicted prisoner had been refused permission to write to a solicitor with a view to instituting civil proceedings in libel against a prison officer. The Court rejected the argument that Article 6(1) concerned only the conduct of proceedings in court once they had been instituted, and held that it guaranteed the right to institute them in the first place. The view rejected by the Court derived much support from the text of the provision – especially the English text. Article 6(1) opens with the words " In the determination of his civil rights and obligations ...". But the Court held – in what has been described as one of the most creative steps taken by the Court in the interpretation of any article of the Convention[2] – that although there was no express mention of the right of access in Article 6, it could be inferred from the text.

In interpreting Article 6(1) as guaranteeing the right to take legal proceedings, the Court had regard to the principle of the rule of law contained in the Statute of the Council of Europe and in the preamble to the Convention.

The Court considered that the rule of law is scarcely conceivable without the possibility of access to the courts. If the application of Article 6(1) to civil litigation arose only when someone was actually engaged in a dispute over which the courts had jurisdiction, governments could be tempted to remove from that jurisdiction any disputes which it would suit them to have decided in a non-judicial forum.

Civil rights and obligations

Article 6(1) guarantees, then, a right of access to the courts for the determination of civil rights and obligations. But what are civil rights and obligations? It is evident that "determination of civil rights and obligations" covers ordinary civil litigation between private individuals. The basic problem in defining this phrase is to know whether it is intended to cover also certain rights which, under some systems of law, fall under administrative law rather than under private law. If, for

---

[2] Harris, O'Boyle and Warbrick, *Law of the European Convention on Human Rights* (1995), p.196.

example, a public authority expropriates my land, do I have the right to a court hearing? Does the term cover only private rights to the exclusion of public law matters?[3]

From the earliest applications to the European Commission of Human Rights, the Commission consistently stated that the question could not be answered by reference to the categories of domestic law; it is immaterial whether the claim in issue is characterised by that law as falling under civil law or not. Thus, it frequently said that the term "civil rights and obligations" employed in Article 6(1) could not be construed as a mere reference to domestic law, although the general principles of the domestic law of the contracting parties must necessarily be taken into consideration in any such interpretation.[4]

The Court's more recent case law has found a broad range of proceedings to be within the scope of Article 6(1): the term civil rights and obligations is to be viewed widely. No abstract definition of the concept has been offered, but its scope is to be determined under the Convention and not according to classifications made by national law. Public law matters are not excluded where they are directly decisive for the exercise of private law rights. Thus, the Convention has, unexpectedly, implications also for administrative law.

Effective access

Then there is the requirement of effectiveness: access to the court must be effective. A formal entitlement to institute proceedings is not enough: to be effective, the right of access requires that practical impediments must not unduly obstruct the exercise of the right. Three judgments of the Court illustrate the issue.

The *Golder* case,[5] in which the right of access was first established, illustrates the point that access means access in fact, as well as in law. It was for that reason that Article 6(1) was infringed.

> "Whereas the applicant was able in law to institute libel proceedings in the High Court, the refusal to let him contact a solicitor impeded his access to the courts in fact. It did not matter that directly the applicant's complaint was of an interference with his right of access to a solicitor, not the courts, that he might have made contact with his solicitor other than

---

3 See Jacobs and White, *The European Convention on Human Rights* (2nd ed. 1996); see also Bradley, "Administrative justice: a developing human right?" (1995) *European Public Law*, 347.
4 App. 1931/63, *X* v *Austria*, 2 October 1964 (1964) 7 *Yearbook* 212 at 222.
5 Cited in note 1.

by correspondence, that he might never have instituted court proceedings at all or that the applicant would have been able to have written to his solicitor before his claim became statute barred after his release from prison. A partial or temporary hindrance may be a breach of the right of access to a court."[6]

Secondly, the *Airey* case[7] provides a different illustration of the principle that the right of access must be effective, and indeed illustrates the general importance of the principle of effectiveness in the interpretation of the Convention. Mrs Airey wished to bring proceedings before the Irish courts for a decree of judicial separation from her husband, on the grounds of his alleged cruelty to her and her children. She did not have the means to instruct a lawyer, and legal aid was not available in Ireland for proceedings of this kind. Although she could have brought proceedings in person, the Court considered it necessary to determine whether any remedy available to Mrs Airey was "practical and effective" rather than "theoretical or illusory". The Court held that, given the particular nature of the proceedings, she required legal representation for her access to the court to be effective; accordingly the refusal of legal aid in those circumstances infringed Article 6(1) of the Convention.

Thirdly, a case against France[8] illustrates the point, also of importance in Community law, that the individual must be given a reasonable opportunity of exercising the remedies afforded by national law. A decree declaring certain land to be subject to restrictions on use could not be challenged because the land-owners were not notified of the decree. The decree had been published in the French Official Journal, but by the time the owners were aware of it the three-months time-limit for challenging it had expired. The Court held that they were entitled to infer, from their participation in the proceedings, that the outcome would be communicated to each of them "without their having to peruse the Official Journal for months or years on end".

3. Access to national courts for the enforcement of Convention rights

In contrast to EC law, the Convention was not incorporated into the law of the United Kingdom, or of certain other contracting States, and

---

6 Harris, O'Boyle and Warbrick, *op. cit.*, p.197. The right of access to a solicitor was subsequently recognised in English law as being part of the right of access to the courts themselves: see note 39 below.
7 Judgment of 9 October 1979, Series A, No 32.
8 *De Geouffre de la Pradelle* v *France*, judgment of 16 December 1992, Series A No. 253.

could be enforced only by proceedings in Strasbourg. This notwithstanding, Article 13 of the Convention guarantees a remedy in the national courts for persons whose rights have been violated. The extent to which the Convention itself imposes an obligation to transpose its terms into national law has always been a matter of dispute. That dispute may be largely resolved in the United Kingdom shortly, although there may be continuing debate as to whether the Human Rights Bill truly incorporates the Convention.

In any event, the Convention rights are about to be given the status of law in the United Kingdom - nearly 50 years after ratification. This will have profound effects on the English legal system. If the establishment of the new Court of Human Rights is a historic occasion, so too is the Human Rights Act. Yet it is not easy to predict what the effects will be, or even in what areas they will mainly be felt. Similarly, 25 years ago, no one could predict the nature or extent of the impact of Community law. The Convention ranges far more widely. The transformation in the domestic legal scene which it will engender cannot be foreseen - although there has been fascinating discussion, on a general level, notably in two contributions to public law, one by the current Lord Chancellor, the other by Sir John Laws. I should like to make a comment only on how the legal system will be affected, taking as an example a well-known case.

Ernest Saunders, who was convicted after a high-profile trial of offences relating to the take-over by Guinness of Distillers, complained to the European Commission and Court of Human Rights that he had had an unfair trial on the ground that what he had said to DTI inspectors had been admitted in evidence against him. The complaint was upheld. I make no comment on the correctness of the outcome, but want to draw attention to one consequence of making the Convention justiciable in the English courts. Once the Human Rights Act is in force, such issues will be raised in the first place in the English (or Scottish) courts, rather than for the first time in Strasbourg – otherwise the complaint will be inadmissible for non-exhaustion of domestic remedies – and will, for the same reason, have to be taken on appeal to the highest domestic courts – the House of Lords (unless leave to appeal is refused) in England, the Court of Session (in criminal cases) in Scotland.

Hence the issues will be fully argued in the domestic forum. The complaint will either succeed or fail. Where the complaint succeeds, the domestic law may need to be changed (without reference to Strasbourg), and the provisions allowing for Acts of Parliament to be amended by a simplified procedure may be used - a "remedial order". Formally the new procedure may not be seen as encroaching on Parliamentary sovereignty, because (apart from being provided for by Act of Parliament) the "remedial order" must be approved by both Houses of Parliament. In practice it may be difficult to resist the use of the simplified procedure where there is a reasoned decision from the courts (even if not from the highest courts) making it clear that the Act of Parliament conflicts with the Human Rights Act – and where there is the risk of future cases on the same point going to Strasbourg because no remedy is available here, so that ultimately the legislation might have to be amended in any event.

Where the complaint fails in the English courts, the complainant may of course try again in Strasbourg, where the Court of Human Rights may take a different view. But at least it will have the benefit of a detailed statement of the reasons why the English courts, up to the highest level, have taken the view that there was not infringement of the complainant's human rights.

Before leaving the European Convention on Human Rights, it seems appropriate to refer to access to the European Court of Human Rights itself. Access for individuals to the Court is radically transformed by the Eleventh Protocol to the Convention, which will enter into force on 1 November 1998. Under the Protocol, the European Commission and Court of Human Rights are replaced by a single full-time court. Hitherto cases were examined first by the Commission. The right of application by individuals to the Commission was optional for the contracting States: it had to be recognised by declarations made by Governments, and such declarations could be, and commonly were, made for limited periods, although the declarations were normally renewed without interruption, and had ultimately been made by all contracting States. Cases could be referred to the Court only by the Commission or by Governments: the individual had no right of access to the Court. And again the jurisdiction of the Court was optional for the contracting States: again it had to be recognised by declarations made by Governments, and such declarations could be, and commonly were, made for limited periods. Under the Eleventh Protocol the Convention is amended to provide for mandatory and indefinite acceptance of the right of individual application to the Court.

It may be thought particularly appropriate that the principle of access to the court is henceforth fully recognised in relation to the Court established by the Convention itself.

4. Access to justice in European Community law

I now turn to Luxembourg: to access to justice in European Community law. Here too, access to justice can be considered under two separate heads: access to the European Court of Justice (and Court of First Instance) itself, and access to national courts for the enforcement of Community rights. Under the Community Treaties, and in particular under Article 173 of the EC Treaty, the European Court of Justice has jurisdiction to review all Community measures having legal effect – whether general normative measures or individual decisions. Thus the Court's jurisdiction embraces the review of Community legislation.

Under Article 177 of the EC Treaty the Court may rule, in a reference from a national court, on the validity of any Community act. In addition, a reference on the interpretation of the Treaty – or of Community legislation – may put in issue the legality of national measures, whether legislation or decisions. Under Article 177 the Court cannot rule directly on the legality of national measures – that jurisdiction exists only under Articles 169 and 170, in a direct action brought before the Court by the Commission or by another Member State. In practice, however, challenges to national measures in the national courts, as being contrary to Community law, often have to be resolved by the European Court of Justice in references under Article 177. Conversely, challenges to the validity of Community measures may have to be brought in the national courts, and referred to the European Court of Justice under Article 177. That is so in particular because of the restrictive conditions on standing for individuals to challenge Community measures of general application in a direct action before the European Court of Justice or, now, the Court of First Instance.

Although access to the European Court for an Article 177 ruling is necessarily indirect, not direct – since the decision to refer is a decision for the national court, not for the parties – nevertheless the European Court has always emphasised that the national court's power to refer cannot be limited by any rule of national law. Under the Treaty, lower courts have a discretion to refer, and the discretion cannot be limited. The final courts have an obligation to refer, unless the Community provisions are wholly clear. Clearly the national courts should not refer every point of Community law. In my view the discretion to refer is most appropriately exercised where the point is one of general significance, so that reference serves the objective of the Article 177 procedure, which is the uniform application of Community law throughout the Member States. The obligation of final courts to refer must also be understood sensibly. It is widely recognised, I think, that the guidelines given by the Court in *CILFIT* are somewhat too restrictive. It seems inevitable that national courts will increasingly have to decide Community law points for themselves, especially where the point is of only transient significance, or where the case is urgent, or where there is an existing line of authority in the European Court's case law which the national court can transpose.

The position is different with direct actions before the European Court. Here a denial of access may be a denial of justice. It is for that reason that, to a certain extent, the European Court of Justice has been ready to fill gaps in the system of judicial remedies established by the Treaties in order to fulfil its task of ensuring that "the law is observed"[9] In *Les Verts* v *European Parliament*[10] the Court emphasised that the European Community "is a Community based on the rule of law, inasmuch as neither its Member States nor its institutions can avoid review of the question whether the measures adopted by them are in conformity with the basic constitutional charter, the Treaty". The Court considered that the Treaty established "a complete system of legal remedies and procedures designed to permit the Court ... to review the legality of measures adopted by the institutions".[11] Faced, in an action brought against the European Parliament, with the fact that the Treaty did not at that time provide for such an action (Article 173 then being limited to review of the legality of acts of the Council and the Commission) the Court held nonetheless that an action for annulment did lie against measures adopted by the European Parliament intended to have effect *vis-à-vis* third parties.[12]

Similarly, the Court accepted that proceedings for judicial review could be brought by the European Parliament, notwithstanding the contrary indication in the text, but only for the purpose of protecting the Parliament's prerogatives.[13] Although, on both points, the solutions adopted by the Court were found politically acceptable to the extent that they were subsequently incorporated into the EC Treaty by the Treaty on European Union, it is arguable that the Court's concern to ensure effective judicial review has led it to exercise a form of inherent jurisdiction.[14] However, the somewhat strict requirements of standing

---

9 Article 164 of the EC Treaty.
10 Case 294/83 [1986] ECR 1339, paragraph 23.
11 *Ibid.*
12 Paragraphs 24 to 25.
13 Case 70/88, *European Parliament* v *Council (Chernobyl)* [1990] ECR I-2041.

for individuals to bring a direct action before the Court under Article 173 of the EC Treaty are not affected by these developments: it is said that individuals have the possibility of action before the national courts which may seek a preliminary ruling from the European Court on the validity of the measure.[15] With well-known exceptions in recent cases such as *Extramet*[16] and *Codorniu*,[17] the Court has been reluctant to accept challenges by natural and legal persons to general measures.

On that issue there seems to me, as to many who have recently written on the subject, cause for concern about the restricted access of individuals to the Court – here the Court of First Instance; moreover that Court was established precisely in order to hear cases brought by individuals, and "to improve the judicial protection of individual interests".[18]

It may be questioned whether the criteria of direct and individual concern, as understood by the two Courts, are still appropriate in all cases; and also whether the justification relied upon for a restrictive approach, namely the possibility of action in the national court combined with an Article 177 reference, always meets the requirement of an effective judicial remedy. These doubts can be illustrated in the field of environmental protection, where the requirements of direct and individual concern are inherently difficult to satisfy and indeed inherently unsatisfactory. It would be unfortunate if the recent *Greenpeace* case should have the result that action by the Commission affecting the environment may in some circumstances be immune from judicial review at the suit of any individual or organisation whatever.

5. Due process in Commission proceedings

An aspect of "fair trial" in Community law is the requirement of due process in Commission proceedings. The Court of Justice – and since 1989 the Court of First Instance – must ensure that individuals and more often undertakings, who may be the subject of adverse decisions, and sometimes penalties, at the hands of the Commission are

---

14 See Arnull, "Does the European Court of Justice have inherent jurisdiction?" (1995) *Common Market Law Review*, 683.
15 *Les Verts*, paragraph 23 (at end).
16 Case C-358/89 *Extramet Industrie* v *Council* [1991] ECR I-2501.
17 Case C-309/89 *Codorniu* v *Council* [1994] ECR I-1853.
18 Preamble to the Council Decision of 24 October 1988 establishing a Court of First Instance, OJ 1988 L 319, p. 1.

guaranteed a fair hearing and proper procedural safeguards. Such questions may also arise where the Commission grants benefits or awards contracts.

A good example is the *Transocean*[19] case decided in 1974. It is still given pride of place in textbooks – for example in the new edition of Professor Hartley's *Foundations*.[20] Transocean was not given adequate notice of a condition imposed by the Commission in competition proceedings. It put forward various grounds for challenging that part of the Commission's decision but did not rely on the right to be heard. It was Advocate General Warner who proposed that the case should be decided on this basis. He argued that the right to a hearing was a general principle of Community law and that it was binding on the Commission even in the absence of a specific legislative provision. He reached this conclusion after a survey of the national legal systems, in which he pointed out the important role that natural justice plays in England and was able to show that it also applies in most other Member States, though often in a less developed form.

This view was accepted by the Court, which held that there is a general rule of Community law that "a person whose interests are perceptibly affected by a decision taken by a public authority must be given the opportunity to make his point of view known".[21] The Court said that this rule requires that the persons concerned be clearly informed in advance of the essential features of any conditions the Commission intends to impose. Because this had not been done in the case, the decision was annulled, insofar as it imposed the condition in question.

Since this case, the European Court has developed a general doctrine of what it calls "the rights of the defence", a rather unhappy term for what English lawyers know as the principles of natural justice and what American lawyers call due process. Besides the right to a fair hearing, this also covers such rights as that of legal representation, the privileged nature of communications between lawyers and client and non-self-incrimination.

The principles of natural justice have been extended beyond competition proceedings to other areas, such as anti-dumping,

---

19 Case 17/74 [1974] ECR 1063.
20 *The Foundations of European Community Law*, pp. 56 and 151.
21 At paragraph 15 of the judgment. It is interesting to note that in the later case of *Mollet* v *Commission*, Case 75/77, [1978] ECR 897, the Court spoke of a "measure which is liable gravely to prejudice the interests of an individual" (paragraph 21), a narrower formulation than that in the *Transocean* case.

proceedings on state aid or subsidy, and other fields of Commission activity. There is now widespread recognition of the essential need for fairness in administrative proceedings.

6. Access to national courts for the enforcement of Community rights

The second aspect of access to justice in European Community law involves access not to the Court of Justice nor to the Court of First Instance, but to the national courts: specifically, access to national courts for the enforcement of Community rights. (This may also involve a reference by the national court to the Court of Justice under Article 177 of the Treaty.)

The starting-point for this line of case-law is to be found in 1963 in *Van Gend en Loos* [22] where the Court stated that the Community constitutes a " new legal order" that confers rights on individuals. Ever since then the Court has consistently held that Community law creates rights "which national courts must protect", but the content of that principle has been progressively developed, and once again the principle of effectiveness has been brought into play.

The development can be seen in a triad of cases: *Johnston* v *Royal Ulster Constabulary* [23], *UNECTEF* v *Heylens* [24] and *Factortame II* [25].

In *Johnston*, the reference to the Court raised the question whether, in the field of national security, the issue of a certificate by the executive purporting to be definitive and so to exclude the jurisdiction of the courts could preclude reliance on directly effective rights under Community law. After a number of police officers had been murdered, the Chief Constable decided to issue male members of the RUC with firearms. However, female members of the RUC Reserve were not issued with firearms nor did they receive firearms training. On that basis the Chief Constable refused to renew the contracts of female members of the RUC full-time Reserve, except when the duties could only be undertaken by a woman. Alleging unlawful sex discrimination, Mrs Johnston challenged the refusal to renew her full-time contract and her exclusion from firearms training. The Sex Discrimination

---

22 [1963] ECR 1.
23 Case 222/84 [1986] ECR 1651.
24 Case 222/86 [1987] ECR 4097.
25 Case C-221/89 [1991] ECR I-3095.

(Northern Ireland) Order 1976 made it unlawful for an employer to discriminate against a woman either by refusing to offer her employment or in the way he affords her access to opportunities for training, except where being a man was a genuine occupational qualification for the job. However, Article 53(1) of the Order provided that none of its provisions rendered unlawful an act done for the purpose of safeguarding national security or protecting public safety or public order. Article 53(1) stated that a certificate signed by the Secretary of State certifying that an act was done for these purposes was conclusive evidence that those conditions were fulfilled. Before the hearing of the case, the Secretary of State issued a certificate, as provided for, stating that the refusal to offer full-time employment to Mrs Johnston in the RUC Reserve was for the purpose of safeguarding national security and protecting public safety and public order. Mrs Johnston conceded that the issue of the certificate deprived her of a remedy under that Order. Instead she relied on the Equal Treatment Directive,[26] Article 6 of which provides:

> "Member States shall introduce into their national legal systems such measures as are necessary to enable all persons who consider themselves wronged by failure to apply to them the principle of equal treatment within the meaning of Articles 3, 4 and 5 to pursue their claims by judicial process after possible recourse to other competent authorities."

On a reference from the Industrial Tribunal, the Court ruled that the principle of effective judicial review laid down in Article 6 of the Directive reflected a general principle of law which underlay the constitutional traditions common to the Member States and was also laid down in Articles 6 and 13 of the European Convention on Human Rights. The European Court of Justice thus held that the statutory rule could not be upheld so as to exclude judicial review of the matter, since this would be to deprive the national court of effective judicial control of the decision to issue the certificate. Notwithstanding the certificate, the national court must examine whether the rule had been made for the purpose of safeguarding national security and protecting public safety. As mentioned, the requirements of judicial control reflected a general principle of law which underlay the constitutional traditions common to the Member States.

---

[26] Council Directive 76/207 on the implementation of the principle of equal treatment for men and women as regards access to employment, vocational training and promotion and working conditions.

Another aspect of the same fundamental requirement of effective judicial review is illustrated by the decision of the Court of Justice in *UNECTEF* v *Heylens*[27] holding that the French Minister for Sport must give the reasons for refusing to register in France a coach qualified under Belgian law to be a football trainer. Freedom of movement and free access to employment are guaranteed by the Treaty of Rome to nationals of Member States. The existence of a judicial remedy against the decision of a national authority refusing the benefit of those Community rights was essential. Effective judicial review, which must extend to the legality of reasons for a contested decision, presupposes that the individual may require the competent authority to notify the reasons for refusing him the benefit of his Community rights. There was therefore a duty on the French minister to tell Heylens why he had been refused permission to work in France.

In relation to the entry and expulsion of nationals of Member States, Articles 8 and 9 of Directive 64/221 lay down the requirements for remedies before national authorities and national courts. As interpreted by the Court, Member States must ensure that Community nationals can challenge administrative decisions before a judicial authority by means of an effective remedy which enables the entire decision, including its substantive grounds, to be subjected to judicial scrutiny.[28]

The Court has adopted a similar position in relation to the free movement of goods. Where, for example, a public telecommunications undertaking has the power to grant type-approval to telephone equipment before it can be connected to the public telecommunications network, traders must be able to challenge before the courts decisions refusing to grant type-approval.[29]

The requirement that reasons must be given for an administrative decision to enable the decision to be subjected to effective judicial review can now be regarded as a general principle of law in Community law. The English courts must follow suit, of course, where Community rights are in issue; and there are also indications of an emerging general principle in English law, outside the field of Community law.

The question has also arisen whether judicial review provides in all cases an effective remedy, or whether in some circumstances the English courts need to go further in reviewing the substance of an

---

27 Cited in note 24.
28 See most recently the Opinion of Advocate General Ruiz-Jarabo Colomer in Joined Cases C-65/95 and C-111/95 *Shingara* and *Radiom* [1997] ECR I-3343.
29 Case C-18/88 GB *Inno-BM* [1991] ECR I-5941, see also Joined Cases C-46/90 and C-93/91 *Lagauche* [1993] ECR I-5267.

administrative decision. Doubts expressed by Stephen Oliver in the *Hodgson* cases have raised this issue, which has not yet been the subject of a decision by the European Court.

The Court has made it clear that the principle of effective judicial protection may require national courts to review all legislative measures and to grant interim relief, even where they would be unable to do so under national law. The point was decided in *R v Secretary of State for Transport, ex parte Factortame and Others (Factortame I)*.[30] The statutory system governing the registration of British fishing vessels had been radically altered by Part II of the Merchant Shipping Act 1988 and the Merchant Shipping (Registration of Fishing Vessels) Regulations 1988. The purpose was to stop the practice known as "quota hopping" whereby, according to the United Kingdom, its fishing quotas were "plundered" by vessels flying the British flag but lacking any genuine link with the United Kingdom. Factortame and other companies owned or operated 95 fishing vessels which failed to satisfy the conditions for registration under section 14(1) of the 1988 Act. Since those vessels were to be deprived of the right to engage in fishing as from 1 April 1989, the companies in question, by means of an application for judicial review, challenged the compatibility of the relevant provisions of the 1988 Act with Community law. They also applied for the grant of interim relief pending final judgment.

The High Court decided to request a preliminary ruling on the issues of Community law raised in the proceedings and ordered that, by way of interim relief, the application of the legislation should be suspended as regards the applicants. On the Secretary of State's appeal against the order granting interim relief, the Court of Appeal held that under national law the court had no power to suspend, by way of interim relief, the application of Acts of Parliament. On further appeal, the House of Lords held that under national law the court had no power to grant interim relief in a case such as the one before it. More specifically, it held that the grant of such relief was precluded by the common law rule that an injunction, and hence an interim injunction, could not be granted against the Crown, and also by the presumption that an Act of Parliament was in conformity with Community law until such time as a decision on its compatibility with that law had been given. The House of Lords sought a preliminary ruling on, *inter alia*, whether Community law obliged or empowered the national court to grant interim

---

30 Case C-213/89 [1990] ECR I-2433.

protection in circumstances where a request for a preliminary ruling on a point of Community law had been made.

Replying in the affirmative, the Court stated:

> "... it is for the national courts, in application of the principle of co-operation aid down in Article 5 of the EEC Treaty, to ensure the legal protection which persons derive from the direct effect of provisions of Community law ... any provision of a national legal system and any legislative, administrative or judicial practice which might impair the effectiveness of Community law by withholding from the national court having jurisdiction to apply such law the power to do everything necessary at the moment of its application to set aside national legislative provisions which might prevent, even temporarily, Community rules from having full force and effect are incompatible with those requirements, which are the very essence of Community law ... the full effectiveness of Community law would be just as much impaired if a rule of national law could prevent a court seised of a dispute governed by Community law from granting interim relief in order to ensure the full effectiveness of the judgment to be given on the existence of the rights claimed under Community law. It follows that a court which in those circumstances would grant interim relief, if it were not for a rule of national law, is obliged to set aside that rule. That interpretation is reinforced by the system established by Article 177 of the EEC Treaty whose effectiveness would be impaired if a national court, having stayed proceedings pending the reply by the Court of Justice to the question referred to it for a preliminary ruling, were not able to grant interim relief until it delivered its judgment following the reply given by the Court of Justice."[31]

Again the Community principle has now been applied by the English courts outside the field of Community law: in *M* v *Home Office* the House of Lords recognised that an injunction could after all be granted against the Crown, in proceedings on which Community law had no bearing. The decision appears to recognise that it would be anomalous to treat English law rights less favourably than Community law rights. In this way Community law can serve as a catalyst in the development of judicial protection under national law.

The *Johnston* and *Factortame* judgments, in holding that national rules must not be allowed to obstruct, in effect, access to effective remedies, are of course exceptional. The general principle is that Community rights must be exercised in accordance with national procedural rules – a principle sometimes referred to as the principle of

---

31 *Factortame I*, paragraphs 19 to 22.

procedural autonomy. The qualification which the Court has made in a long line of cases starting in 1976[32] is in effect that, while it is for the domestic legal system of each Member State to determine the procedural conditions governing actions at law intended to ensure the protection of the rights which individuals derive from the direct effect of Community law, Community law requires that such conditions must be not less favourable than those relating to similar actions of a domestic nature and must not render impossible in practice, or unduly difficult, the exercise of rights conferred by Community law.

The principle is not always easy to apply.[33] One example is the rules governing the burden of proof. The Court has held that the national rules on the burden of proof may in some cases hinder the exercise of Community rights: those rules may then have to be modified. For example: where a tax is unlawfully levied, and the State raises the defence that the tax was passed on to the consumer, the taxpayer cannot be required to prove that he has not passed on the tax. Or if a woman employee is paid less than a man, the burden of proof may shift to the employer to show that the pay practice was not discriminatory. Another good example from a different field of the difficulty of drawing the line is provided by the issue of limitation periods. In the *Emmott* case[34] the Court appeared to hold that, where rights based on a Directive are claimed in a national court, a limitation period cannot start to run until the Directive has been properly transposed into the domestic legal system. Subsequently the Court qualified its ruling to make it clear that the result reached in *Emmott* could be explained by "the particular circumstances of the case, in which a time–bar had the result of depriving the applicant of any opportunity whatever to rely on her right ... under the directive".[35]

The case has affinities with the Strasbourg case on time limits mentioned above. As the other cases discussed also serve to show, both under the Convention and under Community law, the individual must have a reasonable opportunity of exercising the remedies afforded by national law.

In some respects, however, Community law goes further, and may require national courts to grant a remedy where none is available under

---

32 Case 33/76 Rewe [1976] ECR 1989 and Case 45/76 *Comet* v *Produktschap voor Siergewassen* [1976] ECR 2043.
33 See further Mark Hoskins, "Tilting the balance: supremacy and national procedural rules" (1996) European Law Review, 395.
34 Case C-208/90 *Emmott* [1991] ECR I-4269.
35 *Johnston*, paragraph 26.

national law. A striking illustration is the well-known *Francovich case*[36], where the Court established the principle that a Member State may be required to make good losses caused to individuals arising from the failure to implement a Directive. It is apparent that Community law requires not merely access to the courts, but under certain conditions the availability of a specific remedy; moreover the principle established in *Francovich* presupposes access to the courts not merely in respect of administrative or even legislative measures, but also in respect of a failure by the Member State correctly to transpose Community rules.

The principles of State liability have been spelt out in subsequent cases. They have also perhaps reinforced the views of many English public lawyers who contend that English law should recognise the duty of the public authorities to pay compensation for unlawful action beyond the narrow confines of the existing doctrine.

Developing emphasis within Europe on judicial review of constitutionality of legislation

The different topics I have discussed seem to illustrate the emergence of a general trend: the developing emphasis within Europe on judicial review of constitutionality of legislation.

Various factors in European legal systems have contributed to a new trend: the principle of access to judicial remedies even where that requires judicial review of primary legislation.[37] In other words, access to justice becomes a constitutional right.

Within the European Community, since it is based on a division of powers between the Community and its Member States, judicial review of legislation is as necessary as it would be in a federal system to resolve conflicts between Community law and Member State legislation. Thus, the European Court of Justice has jurisdiction to review both Community and Member State legislation, as already discussed, with the field of Community law; and national courts may be required not to apply national legislation which conflicts with Community law.

Within the Council of Europe, a similar result may arise, although only on the international plane, where an indirect consequence of a

---

36 Joined Cases C-6/90 and C-9/90 *Francovich & Others* [1991] ECR I-5357.
37 Terminologically, "judicial review" has been traditionally used, especially in the US, to refer to review of legislation; its current use in England for "judicial review of administrative action" probably owes much to de Smith's pioneering book under that title (first published in 1959): see now the fifth edition (1995), de Smith, Woolf and Jowell, *Judicial Review of Administrative Action*.

ruling of the European Court of Human Rights is to put in issue the compatibility with the Convention of national legislation. The State concerned may then have an obligation to repeal or amend the offending legislation.

Within the national legal systems of European countries, the judicial review of constitutionality has developed in recent years, with such judicial review entrusted either to the ordinary courts or the Supreme Court or, increasingly, to a specialised constitutional court – the last solution being preferred notably in the new constitutions of the central and eastern European countries emerging from Communist rule.[38]

In the United Kingdom, with its tradition of Parliamentary sovereignty, the acceptance of the European Convention and of Community law represents departures from constitutional orthodoxy, and it is conceivable that further inroads may follow from proposals to recognise, for example, a degree of autonomy for Scotland – which might require new forms of constitutional adjudication.

One of the live issues today is the extent to which courts – both in judging the exercise of administrative power and the substance of primary legislation – are required to acquiesce in the view that the rule of law must give way to Parliamentary supremacy. The apparent inconsistency between the rule of law and Parliamentary supremacy may be resolved by the courts making the presumption that Parliament intended its legislation to conform to the rule of law as a constitutional principle. This presumption is powerful and is not easily rebutted; only express words or possibly necessary implication will suffice. If it is alleged that the courts' jurisdiction is entirely excluded, even this may not suffice. If officials refuse an individual reasonable access to the courts, or discriminate against a class of individuals, the courts will usually intervene to correct such breaches of the rule of law unless the language of the statute clearly and unambiguously prohibits this.[39] In conclusion, it should however always be borne in mind that though courts, in assessing by way of judicial review the constitutionality of legislation, are increasingly able, and indeed obliged, to require the observance of those principles that govern lawful public decision-making, nevertheless "in so doing they seek to reinforce

---

38 See *Constitutional Reform and International Law in Central and Eastern Europe*, ed. Müllerson, Fitzmaurice and Andenas (1998).

39 See, for example, *R v Secretary of State for the Home Department ex parte Leech* (No 2) [1994] QB 198. where regulations prohibiting a prisoner's unimpeded access to a solicitor were held unlawful. Steyn LJ referred to the right of access to a solicitor as being part of the right of access to the courts themselves. This he called a "constitutional right" which could not be taken away except by express words or necessary implication.

representative government, not to oppose it – and to promote, not to undermine, the inherent features of a democracy".[40]

7. Conclusion

If I try to draw brief conclusions from this broad survey, I think that three themes stand out: first, that the principles I have described have been developed by case law, in particular by the case law of the European Court of Human Rights and the European Court of Justice.

Secondly, that the case law method is not therefore, as is sometimes thought, special to the common law world. On the contrary, the European Courts have taken on, and sometimes taken further, the principles developed in the common law. There has been, also, a measure of cross-fertilisation, with European law drawing on the rich sources provided by the national laws of the Member State, and in turn contributing to the development of national law.

Thirdly, while Thomas More's life marked in some ways the separation of the English tradition from that of continental Europe, in recent years we have witnessed the re-emergence, at least in legal terms, of a European culture.

Before concluding, I should like to turn briefly to the end of Thomas More's life. He was not of course given a fair trial. Charged with treason, he was given no advance notice of the case against him. There was no presumption of innocence. He had no opportunity to call witnesses in his defence. After initially being sentenced to be hanged, drawn and quartered – a particularly gruesome fate in which the victim's life is preserved as long as possible, and which would today be regarded by even the most strict constructionist as violating Article 3 of the Convention – his sentence was commuted from disembowelment to beheading: the death penalty is prohibited by a Protocol to the Convention, if not by the Convention itself. It is reassuring to think that in some respects human rights are more firmly protected – at least in some parts of Europe – than they were in the 16th century.

Francis G Jacobs QC

---

40 de Smith, Woolf and Jowell, cited in note 37, p. 18. "It is sometimes said that judicial review of legislation is inconsistent with democracy. But democracy as it is understood today does not simply mean government by the majority. It implies also that government will exercise its powers in conformity with the rule of law and in ways which respect the fundamental rights of its citizens" Arthur Chaskalson, (1998) *European Human Rights Law Review*, 181 at 185.

Unpacking the Human Rights Act

Lord Lester*

1. Introduction and history

The United Kingdom Government helped to draft the European Convention on Human Rights in 1949-50. The British Government at the time was determined that the Convention should never be invoked before British courts and also that there should be no recourse to the new European Court of Human Rights, which they regarded as an alien and secret tribunal of law professors unsuited to determine British rights and liberties. We were the first to ratify in 1951; the Convention came into force in 1953 and from then until 1966, successive Governments of both colours refused to allow complainants to go to Strasbourg with their cases. In 1966 after a year of interesting debate in Whitehall, the first Wilson Government decided to allow British cases to go to Strasbourg. That was at a time when there were only two judgments of the European Court of Human Rights, both Irish, both in the *Lawless*[1] case. So, at the time when the first British cases began in 1966, the Convention system was fast asleep; and it was British lawyers using the Convention as a substitute for effective domestic remedies, going to Strasbourg from 1966 onwards, that brought the Convention system to life. We British lawyers were also used to developing law through cases and we had a systemic failure in our system in that, alone in Europe, we had no broad constitutional guarantees of basic rights and freedoms, for reasons that date back to the French and American revolutions and to Benthamite horror at the excesses of both of those revolutions, and a firm belief that fundamental human rights are in Bentham's phrase, "nonsense upon stilts".

---

* The Lord Lester of Herne Hill QC, Blackstone Chambers, Temple EC4Y 9BW and Bencher of Lincoln's Inn.
1 *Lawless* v *Ireland*, (1961) 1 EHRR 15.

From 1966 onwards there was a succession of British cases, not revealing gross violations of human rights in the main, but sometimes doing so. They were cases challenging decisions of the House of Lords – our most senior judicial body – challenging administrators' decisions, and even challenging Acts of Parliament. Notably in the *East African Asians*[2] case, there was a challenge to a statute passed as an emergency measure that took away the right to enter this country of 200,000 East African Asian British passport holders because of the colour of their skin and racist antagonism to their settlement here. That was a case where the European Commission itself decided that Parliament had violated the Convention.

From 1966 onwards, even though successive Governments allowed cases to go to Strasbourg, they were implacable in their opposition to allowing it to be enforced in our own courts. That opposition continued; it was very much the politics of the bureaucracy as well as of Ministers. They rejoiced in the maxim "power is delightful and absolute power is absolutely delightful". The pathology of human rights violations involving this country Sir James Fawcett, a wise President of the European Commission of Human Rights once said was the pathology of uncontrolled administrative discretion.

In the late 1970s our judges, unaided by Parliament, began to develop judicial review. Inspired by the influence of European Community law, they became purposive rather than literal in their interpretation of statutes, and gradually from the late 1970s our English courts, began to use the Convention to interpret ambiguous legislation, to develop the common law and to guide them in matters of legal policy – all that with no Parliamentary mandate of any kind. In 1990, in the *Brind*[3] case, they decided that they could go no further when it came to delegated powers where the Home Secretary was censoring broadcasting. They held that it would usurp the role of Parliament if they were to bind the administration to exercise broad statutory powers in accordance with the Convention.

Until the mid-1990s, the two main political parties vied with each other in their hostility to the incorporation of the Convention. However, Derry Irvine was converted to incorporation and in turn converted John Smith. Tony Blair agreed with both of them and therefore the Labour Party, before the last election, committed itself to domesticate the Convention in our legal system.

---

2 *East African Asians* v *United Kingdom*, (1973)3 EHRR 313.
3 R v *Secretary of State for the Home Department ex parte Brind* [1991] 1 AC 696 (HL).

That is a very brief history. It is all much more complicated and more interesting than that. The Human Rights Bill has to be understood in the context not only of its own terms, but also in terms of the legislation on devolution to Scotland, Wales and Northern Ireland because compliance with Convention rights is to be found in all of those Bills limiting the powers of the devolved parliaments, assemblies and administrations. It is to be brought into force in July 1999 in Scotland, Wales and Northern Ireland, but not unfortunately apparently in England until rather later, probably the year 2000.[4]

2. The legislative provisions

Now, I want to explain why the Human Rights Bill is a subtle, imaginative, exquisitely drafted piece of legislation which is remarkable because it recognises that it is a constitutional document containing fundamental law. If you look at the Bill, you will find in the first clause the rights that are to be enforced in our courts set out, and you will notice a strange thing; on the face of it, the Government cannot count: it says that it incorporates Articles 2-12 and 14. It leaves out Article 13. The reason it leaves out Article 13 is a matter we could discuss at very great length. Article 13 is the provision which says that everyone is entitled to an effective domestic remedy for breaches of his Convention rights notwithstanding that the violator is a public authority. Why did the Government leave out Article 13? I think the short answer is that it was worried that if it was included, the judges might become too imaginative in the remedies that they might grant and go further than the parameters of the Act.

But essentially we have the substantive rights in the Convention and in its first Protocol incorporated: life, liberty, free speech, freedom of association, religion, marriage, fair trial, property, education, political freedom and so on, are all to be made part of our law or incorporated into our law. The Lord Chancellor is very keen that we should not use that word. He says that we are not incorporating them into our law, and that the Convention rights are rather to be regarded as like a compass pointing to magnetic north and all our statute law, and all our common law, must point to magnetic north. This is rather a good image of these Convention rights being the compass which provides the ethical standards, the constitutional values that must be interpreted and

---

4 The commencement date for the Act is to be 2 October 2000.

applied by everybody once the Human Rights Act is in force. That is why the draughtsman uses in clause 1(2) the phrase: "those Articles are to have effect for the purposes of this Act", "have effect" meaning in my view, "become incorporated", but no matter.

The Bill goes on to provide for additional rights to be able to flow into our system by subordinate legislation and there are to be some further rights in Protocol 7 which will be incorporated in due course, once some discriminatory provisions involving inequality between spouses has been dealt with in legislation next year. The Government has agreed that it will ratify Protocol 7 as well as Protocol 6, forbidding the death penalty. Then in clause 2, the courts and tribunals are commanded to take into account Convention case law from Strasbourg - not to be bound by it - no question of precedent or *stare decisis* but to take it into account. That seems to me to be wise; our judges are not to be fettered; of course if they get it wildly wrong and someone goes to Strasbourg they can be corrected by the Strasbourg Court of Human Rights, but meanwhile, the judges must treat it as strongly persuasive, and I am sure they will treat as very strongly persuasive also, comparative constitutional case law. The judgments of great courts from Canada, India, the United States, Zimbabwe, South Africa as well as continental courts, may all be relevant and may in some cases be more persuasive than Strasbourg case law because they will speak for the common law tradition as well as to the wider European tradition.

3. Compatible with Convention rights

By virtue of clause 3(1), so far as it is possible to do so, legislation must be read and given effect in a way which is compatible with Convention rights. Clause 3(1) requires what I call "the art of the possible". It does not say so far as it is *reasonably* possible. The South African Constitution does say "so far as it is reasonably possible" and when the Conservative opposition attempted to amend it in the Commons by inserting the word "reasonable", it was rightly resisted by Home Secretary Straw, as it had been in the Lords by Lord Chancellor Irvine, on the ground that such language would not allow the courts to go far enough down the road of interpreting the statute book, future and past, to conform with Convention rights. To an old traditional literalist, that of course is a very surprising command to the judges, because it commands them to make the statute book fit with Convention rights, both in relation to past legislation, and to future legislation, so far as it is possible to do so. Both the Lord Chancellor and the Home Secretary have said that they expect 99% of the cases to be resolved by judicial interpretation. The Bill reconciles the dogma of Parliamentary sovereignty with the need for effective remedies. The courts are not empowered to set aside inconsistent primary legislation that it is impossible to construe compatibly with Convention rights. But the Lord Chancellor has predicted that will only happen in only one per cent of the cases.

How is that to be done? It is to be done by the familiar technique used in other jurisdictions, especially across the Commonwealth, of reading in safeguards that are absent and reading down, or limiting, excessively broad statutory powers that interfere with Convention rights and freedoms. Some might say it means re-writing statutes. It certainly means using new principles of interpretation of statutes of the kind that the Privy Council has been using in interpreting similar constitutional documents in appeals from Commonwealth countries. The doctrine of implied repeal – that rather dodgy doctrine, will have no place in clause 3 and the reason is obvious enough. If you apply the doctrine of implied repeal it is easy to see it working in respect of old statutes which are trumped by the Human Rights Act and by Convention rights - but you cannot adopt the doctrine of implied repeal for future statutes, because that would mean that a statute enacted in 2001 which has some provision which might be regarded as inconsistent would be regarded as trumping the European Convention rights and by implication the fundamental law enshrined in the Humans Rights Act. The courts will require nothing less than express words for a future statute to trump convention rights and freedoms.

4. Due process and fair trial

Let me give you a practical example, related to Article 6 of the Convention, guaranteeing due process and fair trial. In the draft Bill on financial services and markets there is an immunity given to the Financial Services Authority – immunity from civil liability. Sometimes under the Article 6 case law, as you will see from the case of *Tinnelly*[5], a statutory immunity may be struck down as a disproportionate or unnecessary interference with the right of access to courts. This was something that Francis Jacobs talked about in his marvellous lecture

---

5   *Tinnelly* v *United Kingdom*, (1999) 27 EHRR 249.

last night. So, the question for a judge would be, if someone challenged that immunity, "Is it possible to read the Financial Services and Markets Abuse Act 2000 compatibly with Convention rights?" The doctrine of implied repeal will not apply and there is a gadget built into the Bill, which we borrowed from the New Zealand Bill of Rights Act, which will help judges to use a strong interpretation requiring express statements of incompatibility and not mere implications. You find that in clause 19, which provides that from now on every Government Bill is to be accompanied by a statement by a Minister as to whether he thinks it is compatible or incompatible with Convention rights. That is extremely important to civil servants and Ministers, but it is also very important to judges. In practice the Government will never dare to produce a statement of incompatibility, except in a period of national emergency or something like that. In the absence of a certificate of incompatibility and in the presence of a statement of compatibility, the courts will be able to say that Parliament intended that the subsequent statute would conform to Convention rights; the Government told them that it would, in their view, and it was enacted on that basis. That is why, although Parliamentary sovereignty will be preserved, in practice the courts will have to interpret the subsequent statute, where possible, to be compatible.

Clause 3 is one of the most important provisions in this law. If you look at the cases in which the British Government lost before Strasbourg Courts, one of the interesting questions is whether a British court could have solved the problem itself without the case going to Strasbourg. The most difficult of the examples before you, in my view, is in relation to the *Saunders*[6] case, because the *Saunders* case was one in which the Companies Act expressly says that a copy of any report of any investigation by the Inspectors is admissible in any legal proceedings as evidence of the opinion of the DTI Inspectors in relation to any matter in the report. The puzzle for the judge would be, in a future case, how to fit that wide admissibility provision with the decision of the Strasbourg court that you cannot have a fair trial in a criminal matter if the defendant finds himself presented with evidence against him obtained by compulsion by the prosecutor at an earlier stage, in violation of the presumption of innocence and the privilege against self-incrimination.

---

6 *Saunders v United Kingdom*, (1996) 23 EHRR 313.

5. The intention of Parliament

One of the differences that clause 3 will make is that the prime search at the first stage will not be to ascertain the intention of Parliament. The search will not be, at the first stage to discover what is the intention of Parliament in passing the Companies Act 1994, or 2004. The first stage will be: does the impugned statutory provision impact upon a Convention right or freedom? That is a question which looks to consequences, rather than to legislative intent. At the first stage, the judge will not be interested in intention – she or he will be interested in consequences; effects. (I owe that insight to Madame Bertha Wilson of the Supreme Court of Canada.) It is at the second stage, if the court is satisfied that a statutory provision does impact on a Convention right, that it will ask: what is the purpose and intent of the measure and is there an objective justification?

The intention of Parliament becomes relevant in a wholly different way from the traditional way. The main intention of Parliament is to be found in clause 3 and the rest of this Bill. It is giving effect to the art of the possible. There will be what the European Court calls a margin of appreciation, but it will not mean what the European Court means by a margin of appreciation. They are an international court, and what they mean is that sovereign states must be given a discretion as to the way in which they implement Convention rights. Slavish uniformity across Europe is not the name of the Convention. But our courts, as they have done in the past, will defer to Parliament and to the executive, respecting the other two branches of Government, where, for example, Government has thought carefully about the particular Convention problem, which often it does not do, where there is evidence that it was fully taken into account and where the matter calls for special expertise by the decision-taker – for example, where it involves the allocation of financial resources, then one would expect our courts to behave exactly like the constitutional courts of Germany, France or Italy or other courts of the Commonwealth. They will only interfere where they are satisfied that there is no objective justification according to the principle of proportionality.

The principle of proportionality means that the way we deploy evidence will have to change, as it has already in European Community law cases. That is to say whether you are acting for the administration or for the applicant, you will need to know how to deploy evidence and argument about the policy implications of rival interpretations, just as we have done for 30 years in Strasbourg, just as is done in other constitutional jurisdictions. Sometimes it will not be necessary. In a case like the *EOC Part-timers case*[7] you will see a classic example of evidence being given by both parties as to the policy implications of rival interpretations. In some judicial review cases there will have to be a modification of the procedural rules. There will have to be in some cases, I emphasise in some cases, more discovery, and in some cases more cross-examination.

6. Declarations of incompatibility

Clause 4 deals with the small percentage of cases where the courts cannot possibly construe primary legislation compatibly with Convention rights. There they must, in accordance with Parliamentary sovereignty, bow down to Parliament, but they may grant declarations of incompatibility. If they do, the declaration is the trigger allowing the Government to use a fast track procedure to put the problem right by subordinate legislation. Although clause 4 says that the courts *may* grant declarations, may will normally mean *must*. I say that for two main reasons. In the first place, *ex-hypothesi*, the court will have found a violation of the Convention which it cannot cure because the statutory language makes it impossible to do so. The reason why it is vital for the court to grant the declaration in that case is that without the declaration, the Government cannot put it right under the fast track procedure. Without the declaration, the individual victim cannot go to Strasbourg armed with the full judgment of the national court. There may be some cases where the court will stay its hand to allow the administration time to deal with the problem by other means, but in general declarations will have to be granted and will not be discretionary.

Clause 4(5) defines the court which will deal with these declarations to include the Judicial committee of the Privy Council. That is because of the devolution legislation where unless we can persuade the Government to the contrary, they propose to use the large pool of senior judges serving and retired, as the core of the Judicial Committee of the Privy Council instead of the House of Lords or some special constitutional court. I will say no more about that now. It is a fascinating subject of its own.

Clause 5 gives the Crown the right to intervene in proceedings where a court is thinking of making a declaration of incompatibility. In

---

7   R v *Secretary of State for Employment ex parte EOC* [1995] 1 AC 1 (HL).

Northern Ireland where they are going to have a Human Rights Commission, this body will be able to intervene as well. Unless we can persuade the Government to the contrary, we will not have a body like that for the rest of the United Kingdom. But the Lord Chancellor has indicated that he would expect the courts to be generous in allowing third party interventions by *amici curiae*.

7. Public authorities

Clause 6 is very important. It creates a constitutional tort. It makes it unlawful for a public authority to act in a way which is incompatible with a Convention right. It defines a public authority very broadly, in sub-clause (3), to include any court or tribunal – so they are all bound to comply with Convention rights; and then any person certain of whose functions are functions of a public nature – that would include, for example, the Inns of Court and the Bar Council, in so far as they were performing functions of a public nature, just as would be the case in ordinary classic judicial review. This constitutional tort can be invoked only by a victim, and one of the only blemishes in the Bill is that the victim test is defined not by reference to the English public law test of standing of a sufficient interest, but by reference to the Strasbourg case law on what constitutes a victim.

This is a hopeless attempt by the Treasury to cut down litigation which will have the reverse effect. There will be cases where Convention rights are invoked in a judicial review in tandem with Community law or common law, or statutory interpretation at large, when sometimes there will be standing, and sometimes there will not. There will be endless arguments before the courts as to whether or not there is standing, unless the courts cut the cackle, in one of the early guideline cases. At the moment that is a blemish – everyone, every judge, every lawyer, has said it is a mistake, but it is a mistake which the Government will not budge upon.

There is also a limitation period which was written into this clause in the Commons, again for the sake of the Treasury. It is a one year limitation period, but it can be extended when it is just and equitable to do so. No other country in the Commonwealth has included a limitation period into their constitutional charters of human rights, and I doubt whether it is necessary to do so in our Bill.

In deciding whether a public authority has breached Convention rights, there will be another big change in administrative law. As I have said already in the context of statutory interpretation, the courts will apply the principle of proportionality. In other words, that ancient English principle, as well as European principle, as Paul Heim said yesterday, which simply says that you must use powers lawfully but not to excess, that the means must be reasonably necessary to attain the legitimate aim, that ancient principle which Paul found in the Magna Carta, that principle will have to be applied in administrative law, with very important consequences for the evidence called for.

8. Tortious liability

One of the very interesting puzzles in the Bill is, what are the implications of making the Convention binding directly on courts and tribunals. There are some who argue, especially Sir William Wade, with shades of Albert Venn Dicey, that there should be no distinction under the Convention between liability by private persons and liability by public authorities. I think that is a mistaken view. The Convention, as with any other constitutional charter, is primarily a shield protecting individuals and groups against the misuse of power by *public* authorities.

To make the Convention a direct source of tort liability between private persons is not needed by the Convention case law and would be incompatible with its central aim. I do not agree with those commentators who think that clause 6(3)(a) will have the consequence that the courts will say that in a case where someone's privacy has been violated by a private television company, the victim can rely directly on the Convention against the private television company, because the court is directly bound by the Convention and therefore the individual's right of privacy under Article 8 of the Convention must be enforced directly against the television company. That, in my view, is a mis-reading of the purpose and structure of the Convention and of the Human Rights Act which is to be read in accordance with the Convention and its case law. The court or tribunal is bound by the Convention, but it is not required to create new torts based directly on the Convention as between private persons. What it is required to do is to read the Convention through UK law, not round UK law. In other words the architects of this Bill have blended Convention rights with our existing statutes and common law. So, to take the example I gave before, if an individual brings his case at common law or in equity, seeking to extend trespass, as in *Entick v Carrington*[8], or the law protecting confidences as in *Argyll v Argyll*[9] or *Spycatcher*[10], then the court being bound by the Convention will develop the common law and equity or statutory interpretation to conform with Convention rights. The net result will be that the individual's right against a private person will be altered by that process of using the Convention as a compass, a magnetic north, and making the common law and equity point to magnetic north.

This is not merely some technical academic quibble. It is important to be clear that what one is then doing is not creating a direct tort liability against a private person relying directly on the Convention. There may be some cases, and this is complicated and I do not have time to elaborate, where the Convention imposes a positive obligation on the State, for example, to protect the right of privacy in certain contexts, where if the legal system does not, a victim might have a cause of action against the Attorney General under clause 6 for failing to provide an effective remedy. But the Government will then rely upon Parliament's failure to incorporate Article 13, the effective remedy requirement and then there will be argument as to whether or not one could bring what European Community lawyers would call a *Francovich*[11] claim for breaching the Convention by not having a proper remedy under domestic law. I doubt whether such an argument would succeed.

Clause 7 provides for the proceedings that can be brought, and you will notice in clause 7(1)(b) that it makes it clear that you can rely on the Convention either by bringing proceedings for the constitutional tort, or in any other legal proceedings, but only if you are victim.

9. Remedial powers

Clause 8 gives the courts remedial powers, and they are very broad. Any remedy which is just and appropriate. Damages are not intended to be generous. The Convention and the Human Rights Act should not be a charter for gold-diggers, and the goal of good public administration is not served by massive damages claims except in cases of gross abuse. So

---

8 *Entick v Carrington* (1765) 19 State Trials 1029.
9 *Argyll (Duchess of) v Argyll (Duke of)* [1967] Ch 302.
10 *Attorney General v Guardian Newspapers and Times Newspapers*, [1990] 1 AC 109 (HL).
11 *Francovich & Bonifaci v Italy* [1993] 2 CMLR 66.

the English courts are steered in clause 8(4) to the case law of the European Court of Human Rights, under Article 40 of the Convention, in giving compensatory remedies. There is this interesting reversal of the normal English rule that you do not obtain an injunction where damages are an adequate remedy, under clause 8, damages are awarded only if there is no other effective remedy. So damages are to be awarded in the last resort, whereas declaratory and injunctive remedies are for first recourse.

There is a very wide discretion. That remedy for compensation is not as of right but as of discretion. It will fill the gap exposed by Mr Justice Schiemann when he was sitting in a case called *Maguire* v *Knowsley District Council*.[12] Mr Justice Schiemann held that there had been an abuse of power, but that unfortunately English administrative law is too primitive to be able to give a compensatory remedy.

I am not going to go into the fast track procedure because you are not Parliamentarians – suffice it to say that I think it is a very fair compromise between the need for speed and for effective Parliamentary scrutiny. There are then provisions for remedial orders.

In clause 11 we find safeguards for existing rights – that is quite important because we do not want to cut down existing rights. Then there is a special compromise put in as a result of the media's protests, which is important for those of you who are interested in the balance between free speech and other rights. What the Government has done is to make it difficult to get an interlocutory injunction where free speech is involved, at any rate unless the newspaper has been informed and had an opportunity to appear before the judge, and it has urged the courts to have regard to the particular importance of free speech. I believe the media clause to be unnecessary, but it does no harm.

Clause 13 is a concession to the Church of England and other religious organisations. Originally they wanted complete immunity from the Convention. What they have instead, quite rightly, is a provision requiring the courts to bear in mind that religion and freedom of thought and conscience are important rights to be taken in consideration.

10. Commencement

Clause 22 provides for the commencement of the Act, when the Minister makes the commencement order. Six million pounds is being

---

12 Unreported.

spent on training every magistrate and judge on the Convention. That is said to be the reason why the Government cannot bring this into force until sometime in the millennium – sometime in the year 2000. I think that is unfortunate. We need guideline cases sooner rather than later as part of the general culture change. To put it off until sometime in the year 2000, may make the whole thing go off the boil and become rather academic in the bad sense. It is going to be particularly strange as the Bill will come into force for Scotland and Wales and Northern Ireland from July 1999 when their public authorities are alleged to breach Convention rights, but it will not come into force in England until 2000 unless the Government changes its mind.

The starting point for your work is to understand the Human Rights Act. What a glorious opportunity it is if you are 25 rather than 62 years old. For those who are coming into the legal profession with this new constitutional document before them, there is an enormous opportunity to develop our law in the way that it has developed in the rest of the democratic world. The Government and Parliament have paid the judges the supreme compliment of transferring awesome powers and duties to the judges. The question is, whether the judges will return the compliment by making the Human Rights Act work. I hope and believe that our senior judges will do so. We must now wait impatiently to see what happens in practice.

Lord Lester QC

European Law and Criminal Proceedings

George Carman QC

1. Introduction

I approach this attempt to give you a brief assessment of the impact of the Human Rights Act, when it comes into force, on the operation of English criminal law with profound diffidence. I am comforted by the fact, or at least the hope, that some of you like myself are at the very beginning of a learning curve on the subject. Let me say at once that I am very indebted to Mr Ben Emmerson of Doughty Street Chambers who works and lectures and writes with a great deal of knowledge and learning on this subject, but having expressed my indebtedness and gratitude, any errors that I may make are mine and not his.

The first thing to learn about the Act when it comes into operation is that it gives further effect to rights and freedoms guaranteed under the Convention, and as Lord Diplock said in a case in 1981:

> "Rights and freedoms are not described with the particularity that would be appropriate to an ordinary act of Parliament. Nor are they expressed in ways that have precise meaning as terms of legal art. They are statements of principle of great breadth and generality expressed in the kind of language more commonly associated with political manifestos or International Conventions."

Hence the criminal solicitor and barrister and the judge trying the criminal case is going to have to learn a whole new approach to construction of the Articles in the Convention incorporated by the Act.

Therefore, my view is that in approaching the lawfulness of the criminal law in action in the future, the question of construction will arise. Senior judges in this country have already had considerable experience of this area of the law when construing provisions relating to fundamental human rights from appeals from Commonwealth countries to the Privy Council. Those countries I think, with one possible exception, have written constitutions with rights provisions. Many of those rights provisions are modelled on the provisions in the Convention. I want to begin by saying a word or two about construction, because one is going to have to learn a whole new set of rules, a whole new set of approaches and a whole new method of thinking with regard to construction of the Articles of the Convention. The writers on the subject, and those of you who know about this area, will know that there are different approaches or emphasis in terms of construction of the Articles of the Convention.

2. Construction of the Convention

First, there is the so-called doctrine of progressive interpretation. That doctrine looks upon a constitutional instrument giving rights, as a living tree capable of growth and expansion within its natural limits. In the well known case of *Minister of Home Affairs* v *Fisher*, 1980, Lord Wilberforce was looking for a generous interpretation. The so-called generous or purposive approach adumbrated by Lord Wilberforce back in 1980 has not been enthusiastically followed at all times by the Privy Council in this country. In 1993 the Privy Council was looking at a Hong Kong appeal which involved an analysis and consideration of the Bill of Rights of Ordinance, recently then introduced into Hong Kong legislation. They adopted a more conservative approach than Lord Wilberforce in the *Fisher* case. There are, perhaps, three principles of construction of which there is much learning and much debate.

Principles of construction

(1) The purposive and generous construction. The approach there, is that full recognition and effect must be given to the fact that the Act and the Convention are intended to give effect to guaranteed fundamental rights and freedoms. In other words, it should not be construed like an ordinary commercial contract or like an ordinary domestic statute. The cases so far show that this is not just a matter of taking into account different language and context, it is a different approach to construction. Although the construction must not be inconsistent with the words used in the Article, these should not necessarily be read literally and fine distinctions should not be drawn on the basis of whether a particular word or phrase is used

or repeated. The courts should not be over concerned with technicalities, but look at the substance and the reality of what is involved by the relevant provision.

A corollary of this principle is the strict approach to the limitation on qualified rights. Further qualifications cannot be implied into the Convention and those that are present must be strictly construed against the State and in favour of the freedom of the individual.

(2) The construction theory, the principle of what might be called practical effectiveness. The Human Rights Act and the Convention must be construed in a way which provides practical and effective protection for the rights guaranteed. The courts must give full recognition to the terms of the Convention so as to make it work.

(3) The principle of dynamic interpretation simply amounts to this: that the Articles in the Convention, when incorporated into domestic law by the Act, are a growing and living thing, and they must be adapted to contemporary social conditions. After all the Convention was formulated in 1951. The thinking then of the countries involved in terms of the social attitudes of the day was clearly materially different to the social attitudes as they will be in the year 2000 or so. So the interpretation must be dynamic and accommodate contemporary social thought. It does not mean that there must be uniformity of social approach in the countries which are subscribing to the Convention but it does mean that it is an aid or approach to construction which the domestic courts can and should take into account.

In the criminal law, defence lawyers in the courts will be able to argue, for the first time that in some way, the actual criminal offences alleged, breach the provisions of one or more Articles in the Convention. One gives a few examples under Article 8 - we look at the right to privacy - under Article 10 of course, the right to freedom of expression, under Article 11; the right of assembly and association. One looks at any reverse onus of proof clause which might offend the presumption of innocence under Article 6: the right to a fair trial. Under Article 7 one looks at whether the common law offence is sufficiently clear and specific in order to give a defendant a clear understanding of that with which he is charged. In those kind of areas, therefore, there might be a challenge by defence lawyers to the domestic statute or the common law.

Methods for invoking a challenge

What, one asks, are the methods by which a criminal defence lawyer may invoke such a challenge. They can conveniently be summarised under five heads:

(1) Objection may be taken to the issue of a summons for a common law offence.

(2) There might be a motion at the beginning of a trial to quash an indictment for a common law offence.

(3) It will be important and incumbent on the defence lawyer to raise a convention challenge at the trial as a defence to a common law charge. Absent the positive raising of the Convention challenge, one would not thereafter be able to appeal the matter further.

(4) In the currency of a trial the Convention and its principles may be invoked as an aid to construction of the statute under which a defendant is charged and to argue that the domestic statute first of all is capable of being construed so as to conform to the Convention and secondly, that it should be so construed so as to adopt the Convention.

Immediately, at the moment you go into this territory as a defence lawyer, you are raising the kind of problem which is far reaching and revolutionary and extremely important, namely, you may be attacking the historic doctrine of precedent as we understand it from our own learning in jurisprudence in this country.
To take an example: whether in a Magistrates' Court or a Crown Court, one might be arguing that the criminal charge which is laid offends or is incompatible with, or should be construed in terms of, a relevant Article in the Convention. The contrary reaction may be "Ah well, when one looks at a decision of a superior court in this country, the domestic court of inferior jurisdiction should be bound by the interpretation of the superior court". But that will not be so of necessity, because if, for example in the crown court, normally bound by decisions of the Court of Appeal Criminal Division or indeed of the House of Lords, that decision of the superior court in itself offends interpretation compatible with an Article of the Convention, then one will be arguing that the doctrine of precedent

is overruled and to be put on one side, and that the statute should be interpreted by the court of trial in accordance with the provisions of the relevant Article.

It is not the overthrow, but the reconsideration and the revisiting of the historic doctrine of precedent which is one of the silent bombshells which will occur when this Act becomes part of the domestic law of this country. It will require re-thinking of the doctrine of precedent by the lawyer and the judge alike.

(5) A defence lawyer will be able to invoke the Convention by making an application for a declaration that a conviction involves a breach of the Convention. If a situation arises in which it is impossible to reconcile the primary domestic law under which the charge is laid, and a Convention right, then the ultimate resort is to seek a declaration of incompatibility between the primary domestic law and the relevant article of the Convention. As I am sure you know, the practical effect of that, (and that right will be invested in the High Court, the Court of Appeal and the House of Lords), if there is a declaration of incompatibility between the domestic law or statute and an Article in the Convention, will be that the relevant minister or Government department will introduce legislation, and it can be done by statutory instrument, expeditiously, to excise that part of the offending domestic law. Of course in overseas countries where they have comparable provisions to the Convention (and I have in mind Canada where they are talking of little else except the impact of the Charter on the ordinary Canadian law), there are provisions enabling the courts to strike down offending provisions of the domestic law. Of course, that cannot happen here; we have a typically subtle British compromise in the Act by which the court will not be enabled to disqualify or strike out provisions of the domestic law because they are incompatible with the Convention law. We take the side route that the higher courts in the country can make, on application, a declaration of incompatibility and that may or should cause the relevant branch of the executive to produce quick and speedy legislation, probably by statutory instrument, to cure the problem.

3. Review of the Convention's provisions

Article 3: prohibition against torture etc

Let me review very briefly and really just give a worm's eye view of various provisions in the Articles which may give rise to interesting problems for the criminal practitioner. Let us begin with Article 3, which prescribes a prohibition against torture or against inhuman or degrading treatment or punishment. Normally one would say that in this country such an Article is academic, because of course we live in a very civilised society with a civilised system of sentencing and penology. However, there are two areas where as examples, one can foresee that there might be arguments mounted by the criminal practitioner of a potential breach of Article 3 of the Convention.

The first might be the overall length of a custodial sentence which theoretically might be argued to be in principle inhuman punishment, wholly disproportionate to the gravity of the offence. In real practice, of course, that is extremely improbable, but it does in theory mean that there might be an overview by the Convention principles to sentencing policy in this country. It is an unlikely scenario but a theoretical one that I mention.

A second area in which Article 3 might be offended by the domestic courts is the extradition of an individual under the relevant legislation. An order of the court or any public authority for extradition of an individual to another jurisdiction may, in certain circumstances, violate Article 3 of the Convention. What at first sight seems a mere protection of fairly primitive rights, namely prohibition of torture, inhuman or degrading treatment or punishment, at second glance may give rise to practical considerations that so far, as far as I know, have not really been tested or tried in terms of UK courts.

Article 5 the right to liberty

Let me move on to Article 5, which secures the right to liberty etc and security, and one can get down to the detail. It has of course, as most of these Articles have, qualifying provisions to the absolute statement in the first section of the Article. One finds in the second section of the Article qualifying provisions which give it on occasion a more pragmatic approach. Let me give you one or two examples; the situation with regard to Article 5 and the criminal law. The police has the power to detain an individual temporarily to establish the ownership of a motor vehicle and such a power would be respected and not afford or provide any argument that there is a breach of Article 5. Under the Prevention of Terrorism legislation there is a right to submit a suspect to questioning. That again would be something that the police would be entitled to do because it is a qualifying safeguard built in to the absolute right of liberty. On the other hand, the court has held that a detention under the terrorist legislation for four days and six hours was, in fact, unlawful. Of course all the provisions and procedures with regard to bail of defendants in this country may arise for consideration under Article 5. Mandatory life sentences may also arise for consideration. The detention of juveniles indefinitely at her Majesty's Pleasure may again arise for consideration under Article 5.

It may be that in some of these areas the court has already provided fairly effective answers but I am sure that you can see straight away that although these rights are stated in very general terms in the relevant Articles, when one comes to consider their application to our domestic law in the most mundane circumstances, one can see how a challenge may arise in theory, perhaps not always in practice, under the Convention. It may be convenient whilst I am skipping through the potential effects of the Articles of the Convention, to say this: it will be unfortunate if practitioners in this country, when these Articles of the Convention are incorporated when the Act comes into force, over-frequently take bad points on these matters. After all, the grass roots court of the criminal law is the Magistrates' Court and more offences are tried there than anywhere else. So, if the enthusiastic but ill-advised criminal practitioner were to take these points, and on occasion to succeed at first instance, they would find that when the matter went on appeal, his or her triumph was short-lived. It would be an unfortunate start to the advent of the Human Rights Act if too many bad cases were taken through enthusiasm at an early stage. This is going to be a complicated, gradual and careful evolution in our domestic criminal jurisprudence.

Article 6: the right to a fair trial

Article 6 is by far and away the most serious Article in terms of impact on the criminal law in this country: the right to a fair trial. Built into Article 6 is a doctrine called the equality of arms principle. To apply that to the criminal law of this country, simply stated, means that the defendant and his legal advisers must not be placed at a substantial disadvantage to the prosecution. With the problems of legal aid in this country both as to its availability and its quality up for grabs and unknown as to where it is going, save in the mind and heart of the Lord Chancellor, one wonders how equality of arms is going to work in practice in the criminal courts. Let me give you one example. There may be a very technical criminal case where the Crown is able to invoke the assistance of sophisticated erudite experts on a particular field. Of course, under the umbrella of a legal aid certificate the defence will be able to apply for access to a rival independent expert. But in reality there may well be a financial capping of the amount that might be spent on such an expert so that in the real world, the prosecution may have access to top level expert evidence that may be denied to the defence under financial constraint. One can see immediately that in the criminal trial process that might produce a circumstance in which the equality of arms principle is so fundamentally offended that a breach of Article 6 may arise.

One looks again at the quality of representation. I know not what the fees will be for criminal practitioners under the legal aid system in this country in the future. I note the Lord Chancellor's comment, I think after the House of Lords decision on fees, that he was either thinking of or about to produce a fixed scale of fees. Heaven forbid that new arrivals at the Bar will be deterred from embarking upon a criminal practice career by virtue of some serious financial deterrent or disincentive. We do not want a situation in this country where the quality of representation in the criminal defence area is seriously below that of the prosecution on heavy and complex cases. Of course, by contrast, we have a system of public defenders and free access by members of the Crown Prosecution Service to conduct prosecutions, so it may be that parity of representation may be achieved. But I mention the equality of arms principle, because I believe that to be a very important element potentially in the application of Article 6.

Let me give you one or two more examples of the application of Article 6 as to where it may apply in the criminal law: illegally obtained evidence, what a judge, now deceased, used to call evidence obtained under the dirty dogs act. There is no absolute bar under the Convention, and the decisions made by the court thereunder, to illegally obtained evidence, but the court may have to balance, on the one hand, the importance in the trial of the illegally obtained evidence and on the other, the depth of the iniquity or illegality in the manner in which it is obtained, so there might be a balancing exercise there, and if the traditional approach does not conform with the Convention approach there might be an objection under Article 6 to illegally obtained evidence.

Let us take hearsay evidence. Hearsay evidence is permitted in certain limited circumstances with certain safeguards under our existing domestic legislation. The general principle, and I state generally because it may be subject to exceptions under the Convention, will be and is that hearsay evidence would not be permitted, or may be excluded, if there is no opportunity to cross-examine the maker of the hearsay statement. One sees straight away that this may be an extension of our existing law, or to put it another way: our existing law may offend the principles of illegally obtained evidence approached under Article 6 of the Convention.

Let me move on to accomplice evidence. Accomplice evidence again may well be admissible but subject to certain safeguards. The safeguards may be in a jury trial, that the jury are made clearly aware of the existence of the accomplice and the background to the accomplice, but again there is an umbrella safeguard under Article 6 apart from our own safeguards with regard to accomplice evidence.

To take another point on Article 6 – evidence which involves entrapment of a defendant or where the prosecution or police officers are acting as agents provocateurs. One can recall the sexual cases where the police spent their time either sitting on the walls of public lavatories or going into them. Quite interestingly under Article 6 of the Convention, entrapment evidence, or the evidence of agents provocateurs, will be excluded where the circumstances reveal that a police officer is inciting a witness to commit a crime as opposed to taking a merely passive role in the matter. In cases of corruption or drugs or those sexual offences one can see that the threshold between passive observance or posing as a customer for drugs and so on, the threshold or dividing line might be thin between a passive role and inciting a defendant to commit a crime. On the other hand, one has to balance the importance of the reasons for evidence of entrapment and the admission of evidence of an agent provocateur. It is perhaps another area where one looks to see in a rather unsuspecting way whether under Article 6 something may be excluded which we have taken for granted for so long.

Self-incrimination I now move on to as another topic for consideration under Article 6. I know the *Saunders* case, so recently before the court, has already been referred to, and I remind you of what really the court was saying. Where a defendant in a criminal cause or matter is placed under a duty to answer questions, as the DTI Inspectors did with Mr Saunders, and the duty arises by virtue of a sanction, namely that you can be put in prison for contempt if you do not answer, then the view taken was that under Article 6 there is the paramount right to silence and the right not to incriminate yourself which is fundamental to the right to a fair trial, and in particular a fair criminal trial. And so, provisions of the kind which place a defendant under a compulsory duty to answer questions will undeniably offend the general safeguard against self-incrimination under Article 6. Closely linked to that, the fundamental principle of the avoidance of self incrimination, is the issue of adverse inferences to be drawn from the exercise of the right to silence. This again is quite an interesting area and again within the time constraints there is not a great deal I want to say about it. But one can say straight away that the courts have considered this in terms of trial by judge alone. When we come to a trial by a jury, the court will be investigating the quality of the warning or direction given by a judge as to what inferences, if any, should be drawn from the exercise of the right to silence. It is, of course, a fairly recent approach in our domestic criminal law and it may be interesting to see how that area of jurisprudence develops by the application of Article 6.

Let me move on to the presumption of innocence. There are, in certain crimes, rebuttable presumptions regarding innocence and the court has already considered one case where, when a man is proved to be living with a prostitute, there is a rebuttable presumption that he is living off, in whole or in part, her earnings. That has been accepted as a legitimate rebuttable presumption. But generally speaking, the overriding presumption of innocence will require vigilance and scrutiny of rebuttable presumptions.

May I just conclude this worm's eye review by saying something of great importance about the duty of disclosure and public interest immunity under Article 6. There is a duty on the Crown to disclose all material evidence for or against an accused person. That includes, interestingly, material which may undermine or attack the credibility of a defence witness so there cannot be ambush by the prosecution of the quality of a defence witness - they are under a duty to disclose it. This again is a silent revolution in the criminal law. In Magistrates' Courts in this country there is no existing duty on the Crown Prosecution Service to give primary disclosure of the prosecution case. There is no further duty on them to give secondary disclosure in matters that might assist the defence. But those rights to primary or secondary disclosure may depend on defence disclosure where they take issue with the prosecution.

Of course many applications are made for public interest immunity in sensitive cases. They are made *prima facie ex parte* and it may be that that procedure of *ex parte* application may offend the general principle of *audi alteram partem* and the provisions of a fair trial under Article 6. Pre-trial publicity may be very important under Article 6; Convention rights may be of potential importance in the discretionary exclusion of evidence (sections 76 and 78 of PACE); the role of the Criminal Appeal office and its Registrar serving the court and instructing counsel as a solicitor may also be of potential importance, in that it may offend.

4. Conclusion

This Convention and this Act and its incorporation into English law, when that occurs, will provide a great challenge to the criminal practitioner. It will require careful and measured development. It will require a re-thinking and a re-casting of our approach to construction, our approach to our own learning and experience in the criminal courts.

George Carman QC

European Law and
Civil Proceedings

Peter Duffy QC*

I have been given the remit of addressing you, not just about human rights and the coming into force of the new Human Rights Act ("the Act"), but also about Community law given that this Conference is sponsored by the European Commission and is intended to be looking at European law from Luxembourg and Brussels as much as from Strasbourg. There is actually a link between the two, and I hope, at the end of presenting to you some considerations on both Community law and on the European Convention of Human Rights ("the ECHR") to offer some thoughts by way of synthesis between the two experiences.

First, a few thoughts on the substantive impact of both Community law and the jurisprudence under the ECHR ("Convention law") on civil law and civil proceedings. Here I can be brief. It has been a truism for a long time that the impact of Community law is that of an "incoming tide" - Lord Denning's phrase. One thinks of major areas of civil law where now a practitioner and a judge will have to have regard to what is contained in European Community law. For example, it is very difficult to run an agricultural case without some reference to European Regulations. Likewise if one is a tax practitioner, VAT is entirely dominated by Community law. Other areas as well include immigration law, at least when someone has any link, even if only through marriage or descent, with a Community national. Company law is another sphere where the impact of Community law directly and indirectly through implementation of Directives has been massive. Of course, there is the area of competition law, and the list could go on.

Likewise, in terms of Convention law, the impact is considerable. A brief perusal of the Convention's Articles demonstrates the way the Convention bites upon criminal law and extends across a range of

---

* M.A., LL.B. (Cantab), Licencié en droit européen (Brussels)

issues, including commercial law, family law and employment law, to name but a few.

Of course, one of the main ways in which Convention and Community law impact upon civil proceedings is by creating a substantive standard against which the substantive civil law has got to measure up. If and in so far as substantive civil law does not measure up, there will be European law points to be taken. Sometimes the substantive requirement can in itself impact in a procedural context. Some of the Strasbourg cases have, for example, dealt with questions of the scope of the law of contempt of court, the granting of interlocutory injunctions and, where such measures are found to be in breach of the substantive Strasbourg standard, then the Strasbourg standard does impact upon the substantive civil law. But that, in a sense, is probably the obvious area, and it is not the area that I want to explore here. Rather, I wish to devote my remarks to the impact of both Community law and also Convention law on procedures and remedies.

The procedures and remedies of the legal systems of the Member States of the European Union are areas which, to a considerable extent, have not yet been harmonised. Our civil legal system is different from that which we find in other European countries. Therefore one has an interesting legal interrelationship between the requirements of European law - both Community law and Convention law – and the impact upon the unharmonised area of domestic civil procedure. If one considers the way Community law has dealt with this over the years, it has built upon some founding principles. In its early days, the landmark case of *Van Gend en Loos*[1] established the principle of direct effect of Community Treaty provisions, itself a novel and somewhat revolutionary case when it was decided some 35 years ago. This was coupled, just a year or two later, with the decision in a case from Italy that where there was a conflict between Community law rights and national law, Community law would prevail over it: the doctrine of supremacy.[2] In the early 1960s, that was as far as the European Court of Justice went and that itself was quite a radical and strong stance. It upheld the direct effectiveness of Community law and said that when Community law clashed with national law, Community law had to be given precedence. But it did not really go beyond that and say how supremacy of Community law should be given effect to in a procedural sense.

---

1 Case 26/62 *Van Gend en Loos* [1963] ECR 1
2 Case 6/64 *Costa* v *ENEL* [1964] ECR 585.

It was really during the 1970s that the first cases started to explore the implications of Community law for civil procedure. One of the first, and one which still contains a test which is repeated down to this day, was the *Rewe*[3] case. The *Rewe* case was an agricultural case: a German importer of apples complained about the fact that he had faced a sanitary test on the apples when imported, contrary to Community law. The German court referred back to Luxembourg the question of whether indeed this was compatible with Community law. The farmer won. He then came back before the national courts and said: "Can I please have back the money I was charged for these various sanitary tests on apples over a long period of time?" "No", said the German Government, "you are time barred". So the case went back to Luxembourg to ask whether or not he could be deprived of the fruits of victory by means of the application of a time limit of one month. The European Court of Justice looked at this question and gave the following guidance:

> "Applying the principle of co-operation laid down in Article 5 of the Treaty, it is national courts which are entrusted with the legal protection which citizens derive from the direct effect of Community law. Accordingly, **in the absence of Community rules on the subject**, it is for the domestic legal system of each Member State to designate the courts having jurisdiction and to determine the procedural conditions governing actions at law intended to ensure the protection of the rights which citizens have from the direct effect of Community law, it being understood that such conditions **cannot be less favourable than those relating to similar actions of a domestic nature** ...
> The position would be different only if the [procedural] conditions – made it **impossible in practice to exercise the rights which national courts are obliged to protect** ..." (Emphasis added)[4]

Thus, after stressing the principle of co-operation, the European Court of Justice provided a three stage test. First, in the absence of Community rules on the subject, it is for the domestic legal system to designate the courts having jurisdiction to determine the procedural conditions governing actions at law and intended to ensure the protection of the rights which citizens have from the direct effect of Community law. One must therefore enquire whether there are any specific Community rules that govern procedures and remedies beyond the general guidance of direct effect and supremacy. Secondly, any

---

3 Case 33/76 *ReweZentral Finanz AG v Landwirtschaftskammer für das Saarland* [1976] ECR 1989.
4 *Rewe, ibid.* at paragraph 5, pp. 1997-98.

domestic conditions cannot be less favourable than those relating to similar actions of a domestic nature. Then there is the caveat, namely that the position would be different only if the procedural conditions made it impossible in practice to exercise the rights which national courts are obliged to protect.

That test itself was applied in the light of guidance given by the European Court of Justice in another case a year later: *Simmenthal*. This was a case from Italy and it was a case, which like the *Rewe* case, went to Luxembourg on two occasions. The first case was also concerned with the agricultural sector and, like the German farmer in *Rewe*, the Italian won. The case then went back to Italy and he, like his Dutch counterpart, sought to invoke his victory and claim the benefit of the judgment. He was then confronted by a rule of Italian law which said that the Italian legislative provision could not be set aside by an ordinary civil court. He was told that if he wanted to get the benefit of the Luxembourg judgment he would have to take a special constitutional action to the Constitutional Court of Italy because only the Constitutional Court had power to set aside Italian laws and Ordinances. That question was referred by the Italian judge back to Luxembourg on the question of compatibility and the European Court of Justice, on that set of facts, stressed the importance of giving direct effect and supremacy to Community law by every court at every level:

> "... every national court must in a case within its jurisdiction, apply Community law in its entirety and protect rights which the latter confers on individuals and must accordingly set aside any provision of national law which may conflict with it, whether prior or subsequent to the Community rule.[5]
> Accordingly any provision of a national legal system and any legislative, administrative or judicial practice which might impair the effectiveness of Community law by withholding from the national court having jurisdiction to apply such law the power to **do everything necessary at the moment of its application to set aside national legislative provisions which might prevent Community rules from having full force and effect are incompatible with those requirements which are the very essence of Community law.**" (Emphasis added)

Therefore, in these two cases, one can see that the European Court of Justice is placing a different emphasis on the role of the national court to disregard and disapply national legislative rules, including those of a procedural nature.

---

5   Case 106/77 *Simmenthal* [1978] ECR 629, paragraphs 21 and 22 at 644.

We have seen that the *Rewe* test has three elements. The first one is: are there any specific Community rules dealing with remedies and procedures? There are some very important rules of Community origin dealing with procedures. Those who practise in the commercial courts daily make reference to the Brussels Convention on Jurisdiction and the Enforcement of Commercial Judgments, the Rome Convention on choice of law. There are other Conventions which have a Community origin and which have had a major impact on civil proceedings and which are used on a daily basis. In addition to those specific regimes which clearly oust and provide specific rules on procedures and remedies, a number of specific Community acts themselves contain guidance on remedies. In the area of immigration in respect of the protection of rights of migrant workers, Directive 64/221 spells out procedural rights which must be observed in the context of any attempt to remove a Community national on grounds of public policy, public security or public health and those provisions are regularly debated before our courts.

In addition to those specific rules, there are also some general requirements of Community law which themselves have an impact in the procedural context and in the context of remedies:

(1) non-discrimination on ground of nationality;

(2) respect for fundamental rights, including standards in the ECHR;

(3) adequate reasons for the opportunity for judicial control.

The first principle of non-discrimination is particularly important. Running throughout the Community Treaty[6] is the prohibition of any discrimination, whether direct or indirect, on grounds of nationality. The European Court of Justice has stressed that this is a general provision. It has been applied so as to achieve procedural results where there is any indirect, disguised or direct discrimination in relation to remedies or access to procedures. An example is the *Cowan*[7] case where a British tourist in Paris had the misfortune to be mugged as he was coming out of the Paris Metro. When he sought to bring a claim in respect of the French equivalent of criminal injuries compensation, he found himself confronted by the rule that one could only do so if one were resident in France, which he was not. The question was: was that

---

6 Described by Advocate General Francis Jacobs in his masterly opinion in the *Phil Collins* case, Case C-92/92 *Phil Collins* [1993] ECR I-5145 as the "leit motif" of Community law.
7 Case 186/87 *Cowan* [1989] ECR 195.

procedural bar one which was compatible with Community law? The answer from the European Court of Justice was: No, it was not because in practice there were going to be more French people resident in France than people from other European Member States. This therefore constituted indirect discrimination on grounds of nationality and the procedural rule had to be overridden. To like effect, the pop star Phil Collins and Sir Cliff Richard prevailed when they were complaining about limitations in Germany on the benefit of access to certain intellectual property rights protecting performances of their works. Again the European Court of Justice stressed that a rule which, when one applies it in practice is going to disadvantage those from other Member States, falls foul of the general principle that there should be no discrimination on grounds of nationality.

The second general principle referred to above and which is often mentioned in the case law (although not that many cases have actually turned on the application of principle) is that where Community rights are in issue, there must be respect for fundamental rights. By "fundamental rights", reference is made to the ECHR.[8]

The third general principle relates to the nature of proceedings. The European Court of Justice has spelt out in the *Heylens*[9] case, in the context of an itinerant football trainer from Belgium who went to France, that there needs to be access to sufficient reasons for a decision that impacts upon the enjoyment of one's Community rights and thereafter sufficient access to a judicial remedy in order to protect those rights.

Therefore, what one has at that first level is both specific rules of procedures and also some general principles of Community law which create important criteria which can be invoked in the context of procedures and remedies. In fact most of the cases (touching upon procedures and remedies) which have been decided in the 25 years of our membership of the Community have been decided either on the basis of specific rules or on the basis of the general principles mentioned above. One of the leading examples is *Fitzgerald* v *Williams*[10] concerning security for costs where the Court of Appeal held such an order may constitute indirect discrimination, in so far as it disadvantaged non-resident EC nationals.

There are relatively few cases that have gone on to look at the other points. Concerning the question of insufficient protection for a

---

8   The leading case is Case C-260/89 *ERT* [1991] ECR I-2925.
9   Case 222/86 *Heylens* [1987] ECR 4097.
10   [1996] 2 All ER 171.

comparable domestic right or the rider of impossible practice to enforce your community right, there have been a few examples but they are really ones that you can count, in terms of successful cases, on the fingers of one hand over the last 25 years.

The inability ever to get interlocutory relief against the Crown or the Government resulted in the famous *Factortame* case and the reference from the House of Lords. Another House of Lords reference on the question of no interest on damages awarded by industrial tribunals went to Luxembourg and in both those cases the Court was able to say that the impossibility of getting interlocutory relief, the impossibility of getting full damages including interest, did constitute a barrier incompatible with the test for what needed to be provided by way of remedies and procedure to ensure the effectiveness of Community law. But such cases are rare, and they have been rare from other jurisdictions, and in fact what one has seen is that over the years it is the *Rewe* test, rather than the *Simmenthal* test, which is applied when one gets down to questions of control of remedies beyond those that are of a discriminatory character. This is not surprising because, provided one can knock out any discrimination, direct or indirect on grounds of nationality, provided that one can make sure that someone from another Member State is equally treated, with a British company or a British national litigating before our courts, it is only in extreme cases that there should be a concern about the procedures and remedies and, to a large extent, procedures and remedies can be left to national law to handle.

In relation to the Convention, the Convention does not dictate to contracting States how they ensure respect for fundamental rights:

> "...neither Art. 13 nor the Convention in general lays down for the Contracting States any given manner for ensuring their internal law the effective implementation of any of the provisions of the Convention."[11]

However:

> "By substituting the words 'shall secure' for the words 'undertake to secure' in the text of Art. 1, the drafters of the Convention also intended to make it clear that the rights and freedoms set out in Section I would be directly secure to anyone within the jurisdiction of the Contracting States. That intention finds a particularly faithful reflection in those instances where the Convention has been incorporated into domestic law."[12]

---

11 *Swedish Engine Drivers Union* (1976) 1 EHRR 617 at paragraph 50.
12 *Ireland* v *UK*, 1 EHRR 25 at paragraph 239.

But nevertheless the Court of Human Rights has stressed that whilst it does not dictate to States how they should give effect to fundamental rights, the Convention does require that the rights should be directly secured and that they should be made effective.

This can be seen in the principles applied in construing the Convention, namely effectiveness and dynamic interpretation which are the principles that one applies when asking whether you have directly secured, in the jurisdiction, the rights in question. Some of the substantive provisions of the Convention contain implicit procedural requirements. An example is the *Klass* cases[13] concerning Article 8 on the protection of privacy, where the Court of Human Rights stressed that when one is judging an interference with privacy, when one makes an assessment as to whether an interference is one which is necessary in a democratic society, it may be necessary to look and check whether there are "adequate and effective safeguards against abuse". That is an area where the substance of the Convention test on looking at whether the right balance has been struck directs the judge and the lawyer towards looking at the domestic procedures, the domestic remedies in order to see that there are sufficient safeguards and checks against abuse. But the Convention provision of most significance is Article 6 and, in the case of civil proceedings as opposed to criminal proceedings, it is Article 6(1) of the Convention alone which is crucially important, because Article 6(2) and 6(3) only apply to criminal charges.

Of the various aspects of Article 6, there are many one could discuss. It covers the public nature of the hearing, the independence of the Tribunal, the scope of the examination of the case, the concept of a trial within a reasonable time. The aspect which has most potential for raising challenges in the context of our rules of court is the right of access to the court itself. The right of access to the court is not, as such, spelt out in Article 6 of the Convention, but in a 1975 judgment, the *Golder*[14] case concerning a prisoner, the Court of Human Rights held that the right of access was implicit in the right to a fair hearing, that it implied that one must be able to bring one's case to court.

There have been some cases where this has been applied in order to overcome procedural obstacles and difficulties that were faced. A prominent example, again from about 20 years ago, was the *Airey* v *Ireland*[15] case. Mrs Airey had a violent drunken husband at a time when

---

13 *Klass*, (1978) 2 EHRR 214.
14 1 EHRR 524.
15 2 EHRR 305.

in the Republic of Ireland there was no possibility of divorce whatsoever due to a constitutional prohibition. The main remedy for someone in Mrs Airey's position as a battered wife was to seek judicial separation. The problem was that the procedure to get judicial separation in the early 1970s was horrendously complicated, reserved to the Irish High Court and involved a procedure which was described at the time as "Byzantine in the extreme". There was no real prospect of a litigant in person finding their way through those procedures and there was, at the time, no legal aid and the cost of instructing a junior barrister to assist in getting a straight forward judicial separation was estimated 25 years ago as being in those days in excess of £2,500 which, if one were an impoverished woman like Mrs Airey, was an impossible sum. The question was: had she been denied her right of access to the court? The Court of Human Rights said: Yes. It held that this was a breach of Article 6 but it went out of its way to stress that it was not saying to Ireland that it must necessarily introduce a new legal aid system but what it was saying was that the result needed to be achieved of ensuring access to justice to someone like Mrs Airey. But the choice of whether this was done by simplification of procedure, by introduction of legal aid or by any other technique was one which was left to the State to determine in the light of the judgment.

Subsequently the Court has clarified the principles to be applied when one is dealing with challenges to procedural rules based upon the right of access to the court. In the *Fayed* v *United Kingdom*[16] case the Court of Human Rights stated the relevant principles as follows:[17]

> "(a) The right of access to the courts secured by Art. 6(1) is not **absolute but may be subject to limitations**; these are permitted by implication since the right of access by its very nature calls for regulation by the State, regulation which may vary in time and in place according to the needs and resources of the community and of individuals'.
>
> (b) In laying down such regulation, the **Contracting States enjoy a certain margin of appreciation**, but the final decision as to observance of the Convention's requirements rests with the Court. It must be satisfied that **the limitations applied do not restrict or reduce the access left to the individual in such a way or to such an extent that the very essence of the right is impaired**.
>
> (c) Furthermore, **a limitation will not be compatible with Art. 6(1) if it does not pursue a legitimate aim and if there is not a reasonable**

---

16 (1994) 18 EHRR 393.
17 At paragraph 65.

> **relationship of proportionality between the means employed and the aim sought to be achieved**.
>
> These principles reflect the process, inherent in the Court's task under the Convention, of **striking a fair balance between the demands of the general interests of the community and the requirements of the protection of the individual's fundamental rights**."

There are shades also of the final phraseology of the European Court of Justice in the *Rewe* case, namely that one must not destroy the essence of the right.

One can anticipate that when the Human Rights Act is brought into force, there will be many instances of applications being made by persons who do not like a particular restrictive rule in the Civil Procedure Rules saying that this is a denial of their right of access to the Court, that being shut out by summary judgment, that by facing a massive order for security for costs, or anything of that nature, that they are being denied the right of access to the court. There is a danger that bad points will be taken. The courts will have to assess whether there is a real case of injustice and whether, applying the criteria that one gets from a case like Fayed, there is a case for real intervention. As the Court said in *Fayed*, what is essential is striking a fair balance between the demands of the general interests of the community and the requirements of the protection of individuals' fundamental human rights. Certainly it has been my experience in appearing before the Court of Human Rights that unless one has a fairly compelling case of unfair balance and injustice, one is not going to get very far and that the Court, in referring to a fair balance, is stating that there is a check to be applied, but a check that is not to be applied in too routine a manner as to overturn normal administrative rules, normal checks and balances. Also, in the context of litigation, it must be borne in mind that most of the elements in the procedural rules are there to protect the interest of all the parties to litigation and not just the party who does not like a procedural rule and is invoking the criteria of the Convention to challenge it.

One must also take into account the other party to the litigation who may have a strong case and may say, "I am entitled to summary judgment in my favour", or who may have a case which is assessed as so strong that there ought to be an order made for security for costs in the event that the other side wishes to pursue it. All the parties to litigation enjoy equally the right of access to the court and the right of access to the full remedy under Article 6, which includes the right to a determination within a reasonable time, as speedily as possible. Also if some of the procedural limits were to be too readily overridden by application of the test in *Fayed*, one could get into the position of delay building up in the dealing with cases which itself would raise a question under Article 6 of the Convention. So, I do see there being considerable scope and considerable likelihood of this test being debated when the Human Rights Act comes into force, although it is likely that the volume of cases where in fact procedural rules will be dissapplied by applying the test, will be relatively few.

I have mentioned that in relation to Community law, despite more than 25 years of applicability under the terms of the European Communities Act, with its very strong priority given to the Community rights, there have been relatively few examples of national procedural rules in this country having to be overridden, and those that were overridden, were done so, in the main, on application of the non-discrimination principle. There have been others where the point has been run, but it has been run unsuccessfully. It is always dangerous to "crystal ball gaze" when an Act has yet to complete its passage through Parliament, still yet be brought into force. But if I do crystal ball gaze, I would anticipate that although there will be many cases brought on procedural challenges, there will be relatively few where those challenges will, on examination, prove to be well founded applying the test referred to above.

Finally, I wish to draw attention to a very important point. It is important that civil practitioners are aware that the national distinction between what is civil and what is criminal is not decisive for ECHR purposes. This, I think, is a potentially very important point indeed. We have had a number of cases in Strasbourg where things that have been classified as civil for national purposes, have been classified as criminal for the purposes of the Court of Human Rights. An example is the *Benham*[18] case, concerning an individual who faced civil proceedings for non-payment of a community charge. This is classified as "civil" under domestic law but classified as criminal for the purposes of human rights protection. The Court of Human Rights said that domestic classification was of "relative weight and serves only as a starting point". Attention is particularly paid to the "nature of the proceedings" and the "severity of the maximum penalty" in issue – not the actual penalty, but the maximum penalty. Because such

---

18 (1996) 22 EHRR 293.

proceedings were classified as criminal and, as there was no legal aid for such actions in accordance with Article 6(3) of the Convention, a violation was found.

The *Schmautzer* v *Austria*[19] case shows how strongly this principle applies. When one is in a purely civil law context, particularly dealing with regulatory actions of Government and administrative authorities, the Court of Human Rights in recent years has been quite ready to accept that a loose control by way of judicial review suffices over administrative action in the planning context and elsewhere. But once a matter is classified as criminal, such an approach is rejected. The Schmautzer case concerned motoring violations in Austria that had previously been criminal but had been classified as administrative in character under an attempt to reduce criminality and to de-criminalise that which would not necessarily be classified as criminal. But the Court of Human Rights, applying a consistent line of case law, said that the nature of the offence and the nature of the penalty was such that it had to be classified as criminal and that therefore the review that was exercised by the courts over the award of traffic penalties, which did not amount to a full review of fact and law, was incompatible with the requirements of the Convention.

Competition law is going to be an area where our courts acquire increasing competence as a result of the Act making its way through Parliament. In the competition sector the potential penalties that are involved are large. The seriousness of the issue, from the point of view of the companies concerned is grave. There is one competition case that went to the Court of Human Rights, but ultimately settled before the hearing, from France where the French courts had regarded fines for breach of the competition rules as administrative in character, and yet the Commission of Human Rights unanimously said that these are to be regarded as criminal. When you are talking about potential penalties of a percentage of a company's turnover, that is a serious matter. It is insufficient just to have the guarantees that you would have in civil cases. In such cases it is important that there should be the full guarantees of criminal procedure, including full examination of the facts, of the law and the like. I would anticipate that when the Human Rights Act takes force, that one of the things that civil practitioners are going to have to be vigilant about is properly determining the borderline between what is truly civil and what, because of its

---

19 (1995) 21 EHRR 511, paragraph 36.

seriousness, should be classified as criminal and therefore triggering the much stronger guarantees of judicial protection of rights of the defence appropriate in a criminal context.

We live in very interesting times. I hope that in this brief survey I demonstrated some of the ways in which civil proceedings are likely to be affected when the Human Rights Act takes full force.

Peter Duffy QC

· A Judicial Perspective ·

Sir Robert Walker*

This conference has already heard some profound and stimulating analysis of the principles underlying the European Convention on Human Rights and the jurisprudence of both the European Court of Human Rights and the European Court of Justice. I would like to concentrate on a few particular topics which are likely to be of practical importance, and of practical concern to judges and advocates, during the next few years.

The crucial articles of the Convention and the First Protocol, other than Article 13 of the Convention, are to be incorporated into domestic law by the Human Rights Act. Lord Lester has already explained the constitutional complexities which have led Parliament, like a superstitious hotelier, to shun Article 13. Incorporation into domestic law has been foreseen and to some extent anticipated by the English courts. In a speech in the House of Lords on 3 July 1996[1] the Lord Chief Justice, Lord Bingham, enumerated six respects in which domestic proceedings have already been influenced by the Convention. The points are by now well known and I need not repeat them. The overall effect is that English courts have, so far as they can, consciously aligned themselves in order to ease the process of incorporation.

1. Exhaustion of domestic remedies

Nevertheless it seems likely that the coming into force of the Human Rights Act will produce at least a minor tidal wave of Convention-driven points. Some will be raised in litigation which would have happened in any event, and others will generate new litigation. The incorporation of

---

* A Lord Justice of Appeal. I am very grateful to the Hon. Hilary Winstone for her research and help in preparing this lecture
1 Cols. 1465-67; see also Lord Bingham's Earl Grey Memorial Lecture, 29 January 1998

the Convention will give new importance to the requirement for exhaustion of domestic remedies. At about the same time the civil justice system will be coming to terms with major reforms including new restrictions on appeals (as of right) to the Court of Appeal. Those restrictions will limit the number of levels at which the average litigant can expect his or her case to be heard and will to that extent reduce the scope of domestic remedies. Conceivably the restrictions on appeals might themselves be attacked under Article 6 of the Convention, although I would regard that sort of challenge as very unlikely to succeed.

2. Rights to court access

The rights which Article 6(1) confers on a litigant or would-be litigant can, on the most pedestrian analysis, be seen to have two components:

> (1) the right of access to an independent and impartial tribunal, established by law, for the determination of his or her civil rights or obligations; and
> (2) the right to a fair and public hearing, without unreasonable delay, by that tribunal.

The first of the particular topics which I want to look at is the litigant or would-be litigant who is particularly disadvantaged, or at any rate feels particularly disadvantaged, in getting to court at all. This covers a wide field, including prisoners, mental patients, vexatious litigants, bankrupts and – widest of all – the legion of individuals who have grievances but are neither well off nor articulate nor influential. That leads on to legal aid and court fees, which I shall consider separately as the second topic. Finally I want to consider the attitude which the European Court of Human Rights and the European Court of Justice have taken towards judicial review and other analogous procedures in which the High Court may hear an appeal on a point of law only from a fact-finding tribunal which sits in private (if it sits at all).

Imprisoned offenders and patients in secure mental hospitals may not be deprived of their essential rights to access to the courts to pursue civil claims, although some procedural limitations are acceptable.[2] In *Ashingdane*[3] the European Court of Human Rights said that:

---

2 *Golder* v *United Kingdom* (1975) 1 EHRR 524 (prisoner); *Ashingdane* v *United Kingdom* (1985) 7 EHRR 528 (mental patient); *J T* v *United Kingdom* App No 26494/95 before the Commission (mental patient).
3 At 547/8.

> "the limitations applied must not restrict or reduce the access left to the individual in such a way or to such an extent that the very essence of the right is impaired."

The fact that an individual has been "sectioned" under the Mental Health Act 1983 does not automatically remove that individual's personal autonomy, including the capacity to give or withhold consent to invasive medical treatment, and the capacity to be a party to proceedings in which the court is asked to sanction such treatment. The Court of Appeal has recently laid down guidelines for such cases which are, I believe, imbued with the spirit of the Convention, although they do not in terms refer to it.[4]

Not all Convention countries permit litigants to appear in person in their higher courts; indeed my impression is that the majority do not do so. In that respect at least England has a more liberal (or user-friendly) regime than many other Convention countries; and every student of the law of succession knows of the case in which Colonel Wintle, having lost at first instance and in the Court of Appeal (and having in the meantime gone to prison for a physical assault on the defendant) succeeded as a litigant in person in the House of Lords.[5]

All our courts, at every level, do their best to assist litigants in person. The litigant in person may address the court at length, or only very briefly, but in either case the judge or judges will have read all the papers carefully in order to understand the matter and see what merits the litigant's case has. Nevertheless it would be unrealistic (as well as disparaging of qualified and experienced legal practitioners) to suggest that the average litigant in person is not at a serious disadvantage in all but the simplest litigation.

In *Airey* v *Ireland*[6] Mrs Airey wished to petition for judicial separation in the Irish High Court but could not afford to engage a lawyer, nor could she obtain legal aid for civil proceedings. The European Court of Human Rights referred to the possibility of her appearing in person but regarded that as by no means conclusive:[7]

> "The Convention is intended to guarantee not rights that are theoretical or illusory but rights that are practical and effective."

and after a reference to criminal legal aid in Article 6(3)(c):

---

4   *R* v *Collins ex parte S* [1998] 3 All ER 673.
5   *Wintle* v *Nye* [1959] 1 WLR 284.
6   (1979) 2 EHRR 305.
7   At 314.

"However, despite the absence of a similar clause for civil litigation, Article 6(1) may sometimes compel the State to provide for the assistance of a lawyer when such assistance proves indispensable for an effective access to court either because legal representation is rendered compulsory, as is done by the domestic law of certain contracting states for various types of litigation, or by reason of the complexity of the procedure or of the case."

I shall return to legal aid as a separate topic.

Immigration and asylum cases

An even more basic precondition to conducting litigation is the ability to sustain life in the meantime. That point has arisen in the English courts in connection with immigration appeals (and associated judicial review proceedings) by asylum-seekers, the volume of which led to the withdrawal from asylum-seekers of income support while prosecuting appeals, even though the asylum-seekers were not permitted to take any paid employment. Secondary legislation producing that result was held invalid by the Court of Appeal in *R v Secretary of State for Social Security ex parte Joint Council for the Welfare of Immigrants*.[8] Simon Brown LJ [9] put the majority view very clearly:

"After all, the [Asylum and Immigration Appeals Act 1993] confers on asylum-seekers fuller rights than they had ever previously enjoyed, the right of appeal in particular. And yet these regulations for some genuine asylum-seekers at least must now be regarded as rendering these rights nugatory. Either that, or the regulations necessarily contemplate for some a life so destitute that to my mind no civilised nation can tolerate it ... Primary legislation alone could in my judgement achieve that sorry state of affairs."

Whether or not that could be regarded as some sort of challenge to the Government of the day, primary legislation was indeed introduced and passed (the Asylum and Immigration Act 1996) although whether it fully achieved the state of affairs at which it aimed seems to depend on a new point, raised in other litigation, as to local authorities' duties under section 21 of the National Assistance Act 1948. The whole saga (to date) was reviewed by the Court of Appeal in *R v Home Secretary ex parte Jammeh*[10] but it is not yet over because leave to appeal to the

---
8 [1997] 1 WLR 275.
9 At 293.
10 30 July 1998.

House of Lords has been given in e*x parte JCWI* and *ex parte Jammeh,* and meanwhile the Government has been reviewing the whole of its policy towards asylum-seekers. For present purposes the point to note is that although in the former case[11] Simon Brown LJ referred to fundamental human rights, the Court of Appeal reached its decision simply by a classical approach to the validity of secondary legislation. Indeed arguably the coming into force of the Human Rights Act will make no difference whatever in this type of case, since however widely the expression "civil rights and obligations" is interpreted, immigration cases appear to be one of the likely no-go areas, at any rate where there is no strong family element founding an argument on Article 8 of the Convention.

Procedural obstacles

Then there may be procedural obstacles of a more or less technical nature in the way of a would-be litigant. One such obstacle is an order for security for costs, made either under RSC Order 23 rule 1, or under section 726 of the Companies Act 1985, or (in the Court of Appeal) under Order 59 rule 10(5). It is now clear that the English court's power under Order 23 must not be exercised (against a plaintiff resident in another Member State) in such a way as to constitute indirect discrimination contrary to Article 6 of the Treaty of Rome.[12] In a recent case of some notoriety Count Tolstoy, having been ordered to pay £1.5 million in damages to Lord Aldington and to furnish almost £125,000 security for the costs of an appeal, complained of the damages awarded as infringing his freedom of expression and of the security for costs order as infringing his right to a proper hearing. He succeeded on the first point but not on the second. The European Court of Human Rights said[13] that its task was:

> "not to substitute itself for the competent British authorities in determining the most appropriate policy for regulating access to the Court of Appeal in libel cases, nor to assess the facts which led that court to adopt one decision rather than another. The Court's role is to review under the Convention the decisions that those authorities have taken in the exercise of their powers of appreciation."

---

11 At 283.
12 *Fitzgerald* v *Williams* [1996] 2 All ER 171.
13 *Tolstoy* v *United Kingdom* (1995) 20 EHRR 442 at 475-6.

I note with mixed feelings that the hearing in the Court of Appeal on the security for costs application (which was itself an appeal from the Registrar of the Court of Appeal) occupied six days of oral argument.

Another much more unusual procedural obstacle – but one of great interest in connection with Article 10 – was the case of *X Ltd* v *Morgan-Grampian*.[14] Mr Goodwin, a young trainee journalist, had been ordered to reveal the source of confidential documents, of considerable commercial importance, which had been leaked to him. In the House of Lords the question arose whether Mr Goodwin as a person who was in contempt (through disobedience of the order of the lower court) should be heard at all. The House of Lords decided, as a matter of discretion, that he should be heard.

Vexatious litigants[15] are also a remarkably small category – the courts are, no doubt rightly, reluctant to invite the Attorney-General to apply for such orders – and the filter of the requirement for judicial sanction of proceedings by a vexatious litigant is not inconsistent with fair trial, so long as there is an objective evaluation of the merits of every application which is made.[16]

The overall position about procedural bars to access to the court was aptly summed up by Sullivan J in a recent case[17] in these terms, which reflect what Francis Jacobs referred to as respect for procedural autonomy:

> "A right to a hearing is rarely unconditional, even where matters of life and liberty are at stake. One may have to appeal within a certain time, appear at a certain time, not be abusive or disruptive, file certain documents in support of the appeal and so forth. Having an opportunity for a hearing does not mean that one may not disentitle oneself from taking up that opportunity if one behaves in a certain manner. I do not consider that it offends any fundamental principle to say that certain breaches of procedural rules may mean that an appellant loses his right to a hearing in certain circumstances. The more serious the issues, and refugee cases are concerned with matters of life and limb, the more serious the breaches would have to be in order to justify depriving an appellant of his right to a hearing."

---

14 [1991] 1 AC 1.
15 See Supreme Court Act 1981 section 42, *cf Grepe* v *Loam* (1887) 37 Ch D 168 for a comparable non-statutory jurisdiction.
16 See *H* v *United Kingdom* (1986) 45 DR 281.
17 *R* v *Immigration Appeals Tribunal ex parte S* [1998] INLR 168 at 183.

Bankrupts

Individuals who are adjudicated bankrupt have only limited rights of access to the court – for instance, in claims for personal injuries of a physical nature, or for defamation affecting their personal reputations.[18] Many find it difficult to accept that this is not some vindictive twist in the law, but simply the consequence of their property (including all rights of action of a proprietary nature) having vested in their trustees in bankruptcy. The bankrupt has no right to a fair trial because (as regards property rights) he or she has no cause of action. The same point could be seen (in a much grander context) when the trustees of the will of the second Duke of Westminster complained to the European Court of Human Rights of the confiscatory effect of the Leasehold Reform Act 1967 in relation to their Belgravia estate. Their complaint was principally under Article 1 of the First Protocol (deprivation of possessions) but they also added a complaint under Article 6(1). The Court rejected the principal complaint and had no hesitation in rejecting the subsidiary complaint under Article 6(1) which (it said):[19]

> "extends only to *contestations* (disputes) over (civil) 'rights and obligations' which can be said, at least on arguable grounds, to be recognised under domestic law: it does not in itself guarantee any particular content for (civil) 'rights and obligations' in the substantive law of the contracting states."

Cause of action

The need for the complainant to have a cause of action under domestic law may appear to be a point too obvious to need to be spelled out. But the substantive content of English law has already been changed (in some cases, such as *Factortame*[20], drastically and dramatically) by the impact of the European law, and sections 6 to 9 of the Human Rights Act are bringing further important changes in relation to the acts (or failures to act) of public authorities. In 1979 the Vice-Chancellor, Sir Robert Megarry, was asked (but declined) to make declarations that official interception of the plaintiff's telephone calls – the plaintiff being an antique dealer suspected of receiving stolen goods – infringed his

---

18 See *Heath* v *Tang* [1993] 1 WLR 1421 at 1423.
19 *James* v *United Kingdom* (1986) 8 EHRR 123 at 157-158.
20 The proceedings in the divisional court following *Factortame III* are reported at [1997] EuLR 475, where references to earlier judgments in the saga are collected.

rights under Article 8 of the Convention.[21] It can no longer be said that such a claim is not justiciable in the English courts. But it is very doubtful whether the coming into force of the Act will make the English courts any more inclined to grant declaratory relief in litigation between private parties, or affecting private rights, simply because some provision of the Convention appears to have direct vertical effect (subject to and in accordance with sections 7 to 9 of the Act – this is, with Parliament sharply distinguished from all other public authorities). But it does not, it seems, have direct horizontal effect.[22]

3. Legal aid and court fees

The future of civil legal aid is still clouded in uncertainty, after a stormy process of consultation. But it seems very probable that the forthcoming White Paper will mark a decisive swing away from the existing system in many fields of litigation, including personal injury claims and many types of claim relating to property rights. Conditional fee arrangements are, it appears, to be the means of financing such litigation in future.

The *Airey* case suggests that the complete absence of legal aid to enable a litigant to pursue a claim may constitute an infringement of Article 6, especially if the claim is complex and the would-be plaintiff is unable to act effectively as a litigant in person. A system of conditional fees might be regarded as an adequate substitute, but it is easy to imagine circumstances – especially involving an unusual and complex claim – in which there would be gaps in the system. If those gaps are not filled, in the last resort, by some residual recourse to legal aid, it will be a cause of real concern.

It is perhaps worthwhile reflecting on the position of a would-be plaintiff who, as a result of changes in the Legal Aid Act and Regulations effected by primary or secondary legislation, is ineligible for civil legal aid to pursue a meritorious but complex claim. What advice would a lawyer acting *pro bono* give to such a claimant, and what courses of action might be open to obtain a remedy?

In the first place, the *pro bono* lawyer would scrutinise the new legislation, both primary and secondary, to see whether it can be

---

21 *Malone* v *Metropolitan Police Commissioner* 1979 Ch 344; cf *Halford* v *United Kingdom* (1997) 24 EHRR 523.
22 Compare, in the context of Council Directives, *Marshall* v *Southampton Health Authority* [1986] 1 QB 401 at 412-413 and 421-422 and *Duke* v *GEC Reliance* [1988] AC 618.

interpreted "so far as it is possible to do so ... in a way which is compatible with the Convention rights" – the wording is that of section 3(1) of the Human Rights Act.

Suppose, however, that there is no ambiguity in the legislation. If the offending provision is in secondary legislation (say, the Civil Aid Regulations 1999) it would be open to the claimant to claim legal aid, despite his or her apparent ineligibility, and to challenge its refusal by seeking leave to move for judicial review against the legal aid authorities. As an alternative the claimant might conceivably seek leave to move against a funding authority, such as the Equal Opportunities Commission. From there the course of litigation could follow a familiar path, right up to the seven-judge chamber of the new European Court of Human Rights established by Protocol 11. (That is, of course, always supposing that the claimant's *pro bono* lawyer is still available to help.)

If, on the other hand, the non-availability of legal aid is unambiguously spelled out by primary legislation, there is no question of Parliament's infringement of the Convention being directly remedied by the English court under section 7 of the Act, since Parliament is not a "public authority" within the meaning of section 6. The English court's only course would be to make a declaration of incompatibility under section 4(2), on which the Government would be entitled to be heard under section 5. It would then be open to the Government to take remedial action by way of an Order in Council under section 10. Section 10, together with sections 11 and 12, provides a "fast-track" means of correcting primary legislation and bringing it into line with European requirements comparable to that provided by section 2 of the European Communities Act 1972. In the absence of remedial action, the claimant's final recourse, as before, would be to initiate proceedings against the United Kingdom at Strasbourg. In those circumstances (and because of the non-incorporation of Article 13) there would be no further domestic remedies to exhaust.

Access to the courts must not be made practically impossible by high court fees. That point is likely to be increasingly important with the restriction of legal aid. In *R* v *Lord Chancellor ex parte Witham*[23] the divisional court held invalid so much of the Supreme Court Fees (Amendment) Order 1966 as withdrew exemption from court fees for those on income support, and also withdrew the discretion to reduce or remit fees in exceptional cases of hardship. The judgment of Laws J

---

23 [1998] 2 WLR 849.

contains a full survey of English cases on rights of access to justice. Laws J also referred to Article 6 and some of the decided cases on it, but recorded his view[24] that:

> "the common law provides no lesser protection to the right of access to the Queen's courts than might be vindicated in Strasbourg."

So as in the *JCWI* case, a result imbued with the spirit of Article 6 was reached simply by a classic approach to the validity of secondary legislation. Laws J has, however, very recently[25] declined to apply the same principle to the presentation of a debtor's bankruptcy petition, which requires a deposit of £250. The presentation of a debtor's petition is, he held, an administrative process. The same result would probably be produced under Article 6, since insolvency seems not to be a matter of determining "civil rights and obligations".

4. Judicial review

Finally I would like to make some tentative comments on what is a very large topic, that is how judicial review (and analogous appeals heard under RSC Order 55) stands up to scrutiny under Article 6. The European Court of Human Rights and the European Court of Justice are already very familiar with the English judicial review process.[26] The Court of Justice is at present considering whether the English judicial review process satisfies the European requirement that a national medicines authority's decisions should be subject to review by the national court. That requirement is imposed by Council Directive 65/65/EEC and it has been referred to the Court of Justice by the Court of Appeal in the *Upjohn* case.[27] The opinion of Advocate General Leger appears to give a cautiously affirmative answer to that question, on the basis that although judicial review does not require or permit a fresh fact-finding exercise, it does permit a fresh "*appreciation*" (that is, assessment or evaluation) of the facts found by the decision-maker.

In all these cases the likely thrust of any attack under Article 6 would be to separate and contrast the decision by the original decision-maker

---

24 At 857.
25 *R* v *Lord Chancellor ex parte Lightfoot* (1998) *New Property Cases* 134.
26 See for instance the admirable thumb-nail sketch in *Fayed* v *United Kingdom* (1994) 18 EHRR 393 at 410-411.
27 *Upjohn* v *Licensing Authority* Case C-120/97; see also the decision of the Court of Appeal in *R* v *Medicines Control Agency ex parte Pharma Nord (UK)* (15 May 1998) concerning the form of proceedings appropriate to determine the status of melatonin (a substance widely used to prevent jet-lag).

(who may not be an independent tribunal and may not conduct an oral hearing in public) and the subsequent proceedings in the High Court or beyond (where the process of judicial review, or an appeal under RSC Order 55, will not normally permit any new fact-finding exercise).

There is some irony in the reflection that the informality and confidentiality of the initial decision-making process may have been adopted expressly for the comfort and convenience of the citizen. One example is in tax law (another likely no-go area for Article 6 purposes). The General and Special Commissioners of Income Tax (who now also deal with corporation tax, capital gains tax and inheritance tax) have a very long history, which was entertainingly explained by the late Hubert Monroe in his Hamlyn Lectures, "Intolerable Inquisition".[28] A taxpayer's appeal against an assessment may be considered in private by the Special Commissioners, some of whom were appointed from the staff of the Inland Revenue – points which might be thought inconsistent with fair trial. (That would no doubt have been the view of Dr Johnson, who famously defined Excise as "a hateful tax levied upon commodities, and adjudged not by the common Judges of property, but wretches hired by those to whom Excise is paid.") But the procedure was actually, as Monroe explained, a safeguard to protect the secrets of a trader's profit and loss account from inquisitive neighbours, who might be General Commissioners. The European Court of Human Rights appears to have taken a realistic approach and has not treated the presence of civil servants on an adjudicating tribunal as automatically depriving it of impartiality and independence.[29] But military justice in the United Kingdom has been held to infringe Article 6,[30] especially because of the central role of the convening officer.

The Pensions Ombudsman

Many commentators (including the late Hubert Monroe and also Lord Bingham in his Earl Grey Memorial Lecture) have noted the tendency of the public, if not to wish to kill all the lawyers,[31] at any rate to exclude them from inferior tribunals in the interests of informality and economy. One striking example, which causes me some concern in

---

28 Stevens (1981) page 45.
29 See *EUC* v *Austria* (1988) 10 EHRR 255 and associated cases.
30 *Findlay* v *United Kingdom* (1998) 25 EHRR 221.
31 Henry VI Pt 2, IV ii 73.

relation to Article 6, is the office of the Pensions Ombudsman, first instituted by the Social Security Act 1990. The Pensions Ombudsman may investigate and determine complaints alleging "injustice in consequence of "maladministration" by pension scheme trustees and may also investigate and determine any dispute of fact or law in relation to an occupational pension scheme.[32] His determinations are subject to an appeal to the High Court on questions of law only.

The office of Pensions Ombudsman is a curious creature of statute. The statutory provisions import the concept of "maladministration" from public law into private law without explaining how it is to be understood in its new context. The office-holder has the powers of the county court as regards oral and documentary evidence, but none of the pecuniary limits normally associated with the county court. The present holder of the office can, and on several occasions has, undertaken the investigation and determination of complaints involving hundreds of millions of pounds. And he has conducted those investigations on paper, with a degree of delegation to his staff, and without exercising his powers to hold hearings and receive oral evidence. That policy keeps the lawyers at some distance from the initial fact–finding, but it also inevitably keeps the parties themselves at a distance. In one case[33] the Pensions Ombudsman made a finding of breach of trust against trustees – a finding that can be very damaging both personally and financially – on the basis of written material which the trustees were not shown, and were given no chance to comment on. That decision did not survive the appeal process. The incorporation of Article 6 can only increase anxieties as to whether Parliament's apparent desire to give priority to informality and economy in resolving disputes about occupational pension schemes may not jeopardise the right of pension trustees to a fair trial before they are held guilty of maladministration or breach of trust. Lord Scarman once[34] contrasted the "twilight world of maladministration" with the "commanding heights of the law". In this part of the law the commanding heights seem to be in danger of becoming obscured.

In this country the higher courts have shown an inclination to take account of the subject–matter of an application for judicial review (and

---

32 See the provisions re-enacted in sections 146 *et seq* of the Pension Schemes Act 1993.
33 *Seifert* v *Pensions Ombudsman* [1997] 1 All ER 214 (Lightman J); [1997] 4 All ER 947 (CA).See also *Edge* v *Pensions Ombudsman* [1998] 3 WLR 466; [1998] 2 All ER 547 (Scott V-C).
34 *R* v *Inland Revenue Commissioners ex parte Federation of Self-Employed* [1982] AC 617 at 652.

in particular, of its human rights context) in determining the rigour with which the application is dealt with. Sir Thomas Bingham MR said in *R* v *Ministry of Defence ex parte Smith*,[35] and the associated cases concerning homosexuals in the armed forces:

> "The court may not interfere with the exercise of an administrative discretion on substantial grounds save where the court is satisfied that the decision is unreasonable in the sense that it is beyond the range of responses open to a reasonable decision-maker. But in judging whether the decision-maker has exceeded this margin of appreciation the human rights context is important. The more substantial the interference with human rights, the more the court will require by way of justification before it is satisfied that the decision is unreasonable in the sense outlined above."

The European Court of Human Rights has shown a similar inclination. The *Bryan* case shows that in a relatively specialised and technical context, such as town and country planning, no more than a limited power of review by the High Court could reasonably be expected.[36] The opinion of Advocate General Leger in *Upjohn* – another specialised and technical area – is on the same lines. But on more general issues, with a human rights element, the position may be different. In the *Air Canada* case[37] a Tristar aircraft worth £60 million was impounded by customs officials, acting under statutory powers, after it had been found to be carrying an item of cargo containing 330 kilos of cannabis. The aircraft was released on payment of a penalty of £50,000. There were judicial review proceedings at first instance and in the Court of Appeal[38] in which the lawfulness of the impounding was upheld but the quantum of the penalty was not an issue. The matter went to Strasbourg on various points. The European Court of Human Rights found no breach of Article 6(1) in the judicial review proceedings which had taken place (they were concerned largely with statutory construction). In relation to the point on which there had been no judicial review the Court declined:[39]

> "to examine in the abstract whether the scope of judicial review, as applied by the English courts, would be capable of satisfying Article 6(1) of the Convention."

---

35 [1996] QB 517 at 554.
36 *Bryan* v *United Kingdom* (1996) 21 EHRR 342.
37 *Air Canada* v *United Kingdom* (1995) 20 EHRR 150.
38 *C & E Commissioners* v *Air Canada* [1989] QB 234 (Tucker J); [1991] 2 QB 446 (CA).
39 (1995) 20 EHRR at 178.

However, it is a safe prediction that there is a lot more to be said, both in Strasbourg and in Luxembourg as to the adequacy of English judicial review procedure. The shock waves of *Factortame* are still reverberating. The Court of Appeal has in *ex parte Smith* given at least a hint of how judicial review procedure might develop in areas of particular sensitivity for human rights. In the meantime, we can take some modest pride that in cases such as *ex parte JCWI* and *ex parte Witham* their courts have – before incorporation and in some cases outside the scope of Article 6 – reached a result which is fully in accord with the spirit of fair trial.

Sir Robert Walker

· List of Cases Cited ·

Air Canada v United Kingdom (1995)	70
Airey v Ireland (1979)	5, 52, 60, 65
Argyll (Duchess of) v Argyll (Duke of) (1967)	31
Ashingdane v United Kingdom (1985)	59
Attorney-General v Guardian Newspapers & Times Newspapers	31
Benham (1996)	55
Bryan v United Kingdom (1996)	70
C & E Commissioners v Air Canada (1989); (1991)(CA)	70
Codorniu v Council (1994)	10
Comet v Produktschap voor Siergewassen (1976)	17
Costa v ENEL (1964)	46
Cowan (1989)	49
De Geouffre de la Pradelle v France (1992)	5
Duke v GEC Reliance (1988)	65
East African Asians v United Kingdom	22
Edge v Pensions Ombudsman (1998)	69
Emmott (1991)	17
Entick v Carrington (1765)	31
ERT (1989)	50
EUC v Austria (1988)	68
European Parliament v Council (Chernobyl) (1990)	9
Extramet Industrie v Council (1991)	10
Factortame I (1990)	15, 16
Factortame II (1991)	12
Fayed v United Kingdom (1994)	53, 54, 67
Findlay v United Kingdom (1998)	68
Fitzgerald v Williams (1996)	50, 62
Francovich & Bonifaci v Italy (1993)	31
Francovich & others (1991)	18
Golder v United Kingdom (1975)	2, 4, 52, 59
Grepe v Loam (1887)	63
H v United Kingdom (1986)	63
Halford v United Kingdom (1997)	65

Heath v Tang (1993)	64
Heylens (1986)	50
Hodgson	15
Inno-BM (1991)	14
Ireland v United Kingdom (1978)	51
James v United Kingdom (1986)	64
Johnston v Royal Ulster Constabulary (1986)	12, 16
J T v United Kingdom (1995)	59
Klass (1978)	52
Lagauche (1993)	14
Lawless v Ireland	21
Les Verts v European Parliament (1986)	9, 10
M v Home Office	16
Maguire v Knowsley District Council	32
Malone v Metropolitan Police Commissioner (1979)	65
Marshall v Southampton Health Authority (1986)	65
Minister of Home Affairs v Fisher (1980)	35
Mollett v Commission (1978)	11
Phil Collins (1993)	49
R v Collins ex p S (1998)	60
R v Home Secretary ex p Jammeh (1998)	61
R v Immigration Appeals Tribunal ex p S (1998)	63
R v Inland Revenue Commissioners ex p Federation of Self Employed (1982)	69
R v Lord Chancellor ex p Lightfoot (1998)	67
R v Lord Chancellor ex p Witham (1998)	66
R v Medicines Control Agency ex p Pharma Nord (UK) (1998)	67
R v Ministry of Defence ex p Smith (1996)	70
R v Secretary of State for Employment ex p EOC	28
R v Secretary of State for Social Security ex p JCWI (1997)	61, 62, 67
R v Secretary of State for the Home Department ex p Brind (1990)	22
R v Secretary of State for the Home Department ex p Leech (No 2) (1994)	19
Radion (1997)	14
Rewe Zentral Finanz AG v Landwirtschaftskammer für das Saarland (1976)	17, 47, 54
Saunders v United Kingdom	26, 42, 43
Schmautzer v Austria (1995)	56
Shingara (1997)	14
Seifert v Pensions Ombudsman (1997)	69

Simmenthal (1978)	48
Swedish Engine Drivers Union (1976)	51
Tinnelly v United Kingdom	25
Tolstoy v United Kingdom (1995)	62
Transocean Case (1974)	11
UNECTEF v Haylens (1987)	12, 14, 51
Upjohn v Licensing Authority (1997)	67
Van Gend en Loos (1963)	12, 46
Wintle v Nye (1959)	60
X v Austria (1964)	4
X Ltd v Morgan Grampian (1991)	63

· Index ·

Access to Courts,
   court fees, effect of, 66, 67
   denial of, 54
   disadvantaged litigants, position of, 59, 60
   effective access, requirements as to, 4, 59 *et seq*
   guarantees concerning, 2, 52, 55, 59
   limitations on, 53, 54
   margin of appreciation, principle of, 53, 54
   national courts, access to, 5, 6, 12
Access to Justice see also: Access to Courts
   European law, influence of, 8 *et seq*
   principles, associated with, 2, 3, 5, 6
Adequate Notice,
   provisions requiring, 11
Administrative Decisions,
   reasons for, required, 13, 14
Administrative Law,
   scope of, 3
Appeals,
   restrictions on, 59
Asylum,
   cases involving, 61

Bankrupts,
   litigants, as, 64
Burden of Proof,
   rules relating to, 17

Case Law,
   precedent doctrine, unaffected by, 24, 37, 38
   stare decisis, principle of, 24
Cause of Action,
   requirements as to, 64, 65
Civil Litigation see also: Civil Proceedings, Litigants
   scope of, 3
Civil Proceedings,
   access, rights relating to, 52, 53, 55, 59
   classification of issues, under, 55, 56
   Community rules, dealing with, 49

Civil Proceedings *cont.*
   dynamic interpretation, principle of, 52
   European law, influence on, 45, 46
   harmonisation, lack of, 46
   human rights legislation, impact on, 45 *et seq*
   national rules, prevail where, 55
   procedural conditions, governing, 47, 48
   summary judgment, entitlement to, 55
Civil Rights,
   determination of, courts before, 3
   domestic law, reference made to, 4
   interpretation of, 4
Community Rights,
   burden of proof, provisions affecting, 17
   denial of, 14
   procedural rules, in accordance with, 16
Compensation,
   payment of, 18, 32
Competition Law,
   classification of issues, relating to, 56
   growing importance of, 56
Conditional Fees,
   practice relating to, 65
Constitutional Guarantees,
   basic rights, unprotected by, 21
Convention see: European Convention on Human Rights, Convention Rights
Convention Rights,
   domestic law, incompatibility with, 38
   fundamental rights, protection of, 39, 40, 41
   implied repeal, doctrine of, 25, 26
   legislation, compatible with, 24, 26, 28
   public authorities, acting contrary to, 29
   remedial powers, associated with, 31
Court Fees,
   access denied, by cost of, 66, 67
Court of Human Rights,
   access to, 7, 8, 10
   establishment of, 6

Court of Human Rights *cont.*
  replacement of, 7
Courts see also: Access to Courts, Court of Human Rights, High Court, National Courts
  declarations, made by, 28
  jurisdiction, exclusion of, 12, 13
  remedial powers, granted to, 31
Criminal Proceedings,
  classification of issues, under, 55, 56
  construction, principles relating to, 35
  dynamic interpretation, principle explained, 36
  entrapment, defendant of, 42
  evidence, issues relating to, 41, 42, 43, 44
  human rights legislation, impact on, 34 *et seq*
  incompatibility, declarations as to, 38
  innocence, presumption of, 36, 43
  invoking a challenge, methods for, 37
  progressive interpretation, doctrine of, 35
  proof, issues concerning, 36
Crown,
  injunction sought, against, 15, 16

Declarations,
  courts, made by, 28, 38
Devolution,
  legislative powers, developing through, 22, 23
Direct Effect,
  principle of, 46, 47
Disclosure,
  evidence of, requirements as to, 43, 44
Discrimination see also: Sex Discrimination
  nationality, on grounds of, 49, 50
Domestic Law,
  changes to, decisions influencing, 6
  convention rights, incompatibility with, 38
Domestic Remedies see also: Remedies
  position regarding, 23, 59
Domestic Rights,
  protection of, 51
Due Process,
  guarantees as to, 25, 26
  requirements as to, 10 *et seq*

Employment,
  free access to, 14

Entrapment,
  defendant of, 42
Environmental Protection,
  actions seeking, 10
Equal Treatment,
  principles, associated with, 13
Equality of Arms,
  principle, associated with, 40, 41
European Commission,
  adequate notice, provisions as to, 11
  jurisdiction, transferred from, 7
  proceedings of, due process required, 10, 11
European Community Law,
  access to justice, under, 8 *et seq*
European Convention on Human Rights see also: Convention Rights
  access to justice, under, 2, 21
  background to, 21
  commencement provisions, 32, 33
  construction, issues related to, 35
  criminal offences, in breach of, 36, 38
  domestic remedies, in relation to, 23
  legislation, conflicting with, 22
  ratification of, 21
  violations of, 28
European Court of Human Rights see: Court of Human Rights
European Court of Justice,
  jurisdiction of, 8, 18
European Institutions,
  legality, issues relating to, 9
European Parliament,
  judicial review, sought by, 9
Evidence,
  accomplice evidence, 42
  disclosure of, 43, 44
  exclusion of, 44
  hearsay evidence, 42
  illegally obtained, where, 41, 42
Extradition,
  provisions affecting, 39

Fair Hearing,
  right of access, implicit in, 52, 53, 55, 59, 63
Fair Trial,
  guarantees as to, 25, 26
  right to, protection of, 40, 41
  tax law, commissioners before, 68
Free Movement of Goods,
  principle of, 14

Freedom of Movement,
  principle of, 14
Fundamental Rights,
  effectiveness, requirement as to, 52
  respect for, 49, 50, 51

Hearing,
  right to, 52, 53, 55, 63
High Court,
  preliminary ruling, requested by, 15
Human Rights Legislation,
  classification of issues, relating to, 55, 56
  domestic remedies, contained within, 23
  ethical standards, implied within, 23
  substantive rights, set out within, 23

Immigration,
  rights, in relation to, 22
Individuals,
  remedies sought by, 9, 10, 12
Injunction,
  remedy, effective as, 15, 16
Innocence,
  presumption, as to, 36, 43
Interpretation see also: Statutory Interpretation
  cases referred, on basis of, 8
  dynamic interpretation, principle of, 36, 52

Judicial Control,
  adequate reasons, required for, 49
Judiciary,
  issues affecting, 58 *et seq*
Judicial Review,
  basis for, 13, 14
  constitutionality of legislation, applied to, 18 *et seq*
  democratic principles, linked with, 20
  effective use, of, 9, 14, 22
  European requirements, satisfied by, 67, 71
  exclusion of, 13
  "fresh appreciation", concept implicit in, 67, 68
  limitations on, 70
  subject matter, relevance of, 69, 70
Judicial Training,
  provision for, 33
Jurisdiction,
  exclusion of 12, 13

Jurisdiction *cont.*
  extent of, 7, 8, 18, 47, 48

Legal Aid,
  access to, 41
  conditional fees, as substitute for, 65
  future of, considerations as to, 65, 66
  representation, by means of, 41
Legal Representation,
  importance of, 5, 41, 59, 60, 65
Legislation,
  implied repeal, doctrine of, 25, 26
  national courts, power over, 15, 16, 22, 27
  repeal of, obligations as to, 19
Liberty,
  right to, protection of, 39, 40
Limitation Periods,
  extent of, 17
Litigants,
  appearance in person, 60
  disadvantaged, position of, 59, 60
  procedural obstacles, affecting, 62, 63

Maladministration,
  injustice, resulting from, 68, 69
Margin of Appreciation,
  principle applied, 53, 54
Member States,
  nationals, expulsion of, 14
Mental Patients,
  litigants as, 59, 60

National Courts,
  access to, 5, 6, 12, 14
  cases referred from, 8, 9
  jurisdiction, extent of, 47, 48
  legislative measures, reviewed by, 15
National Law,
  conflict of laws, involving, 46, 47
  remedies available, under, 5, 6, 14, 18
National Security,
  courts excluded, on grounds of, 12
Natural Justice,
  practical effect of, 11, 12

Pensions Ombudsman,
  work of, 68, 69
Police Powers,
  detention, rights involving, 40
  entrapment, defendant of, 42
Pre-trial Publicity,
  safeguards, as to, 44

Privacy,
  protection of, 52
Privileged Communications,
  position of, 11
Privy Council,
  role of, 28
Procedural Autonomy,
  principle of, 16, 17, 63
Proof see: Burden of Proof
Proportionality,
  principle of, 27, 28
Public Authorities,
  convention rights, acting contrary to, 29
  definition of, 29
  liability of, 29, 30
  limitation periods, affecting, 29, 30
Public Interest Immunity, 43, 44
Public Order,
  preservation of, action taken, 13
Public Safety,
  actions to protect, 13

Remedial Orders,
  use of, 7
Remedial Powers,
  compensation, payment of, 31
  damages, award of, 31
  injunction, grant of, 32
Remedies see also: Remedial Orders, Remedial Powers
  availability of, 15, 16, 17, 18
  Community rules, dealing with, 49
  individuals, sought by, 9, 10

Remedial Powers *cont.*
  interim relief, criteria for, 15,
  injunction sought, by way of, 15, 16, 33
  national law, under, 5, 6, 14, 18
Representation see: Legal Representation
Rule of Law,
  legislative supremacy, and, 19, 46, 48
  maintenance of, 3, 9

Self-incrimination,
  protection against, 11, 26, 42, 43
Sex Discrimination,
  unlawful, allegations of, 12, 13
Statutory Interpretation,
  legislative intent, importance of, 27
  judicial influence, limits of, 22, 25
Subordinate Legislation,
  role of, 24, 28, 38, 67
Supremacy,
  legislative provisions, doctrine associated with, 19, 46, 48

Tax Law,
  commissioners, hearings before, 68
Thomas More,
  contribution made by, 1, 2, 20
Tortious Liability,
  extension of, 30, 31
Torture,
  prohibitions against, 39

Vexatious Litigants,
  position of, 63